DEDICATION

This book has been 66 years in the making, and so many people have contributed to its creation. I am profoundly grateful for every aspect of my life—the lessons learned, and all the moments of joy, happiness, and even sorrow. Each day is truly a gift, and life is what we make of it.

First and foremost, I thank my wife, Patti Jo, for her unwavering support, patience, and trust in my gift. She has stood by my side through all of life's ups and downs.

To my clients: thank you for placing your trust in me and helping me grow spiritually. Your presence and faith have shaped me in immeasurable ways.

Special love and gratitude go to Tamara Rose, Tania Rae, James Van Praagh, Dr. Joe Dispenza, Dr. Bruce Lipton, and Tiffany Barsotti. You have each had a direct or indirect influence on who I am today.

I offer special thanks to Alex McCann Johnson, his partner Eugine, and Guided by Spirit Publications. Your guidance, love, and support were instrumental in bringing this book to life.

To Spirit and the entire spiritual hierarchy: I am honored by your trust and forever thankful for the love, guidance, healing energies, compassion, and understanding you have shared, allowing me to be of service to others.

I am truly blessed in this life.

Through the Eyes of an Energy Healer

Through the
EYES

of an
ENERGY
HEALER

By Rev. Thomas A. Lewan, PhD.

GUIDED BY SPIRIT
PUBLISHING

Through the Eyes of an Energy Healer

Thomas A. Lewan

Published by Guided by Spirit Publishing

Guided by Spirit Publishing
203 Main St.
Williston, ND, 58801, USA
www.guidedbyspiritpublishing.com
info@guidedbyspiritpublishing.com

ISBN: 979-8-9913133-3-9

Printed in the United States of America

Cover Design by Eugine Johnson

CONTENTS

Discover deeper insights and personal reflections straight from the author! Scan the QR code to explore the wisdom behind the words.

INTRODUCTION TO
THROUGH THE EYES OF AN ENERGY
HEALER

Our world is a complex blend of what we can see and what we can't. We often focus on the physical things in life and forget about the invisible energies that shape our lives. This book is an invitation to explore energy healing, an ancient practice based on the idea that everything in the universe is connected by a vibrant energy.

Energy healing works by balancing and channeling this universal life force to promote health and change. This isn't a new fad; it's a practice that has been around for centuries. Different cultures have recognized and used this energy for healing and spiritual growth. From the shamanic traditions of indigenous tribes to the practices of Chinese chi and Indian prana, the idea of a life-sustaining energy is universal. Even the ancient Egyptians used energy rituals to connect with cosmic forces, showing that this concept is deeply rooted in human history.

My interest in energy healing started when I was young. I was fascinated by stories of healers who could heal with just a touch or a look, and by wise women who used herbs and chants. What intrigued me most was their connection to a realm beyond the physical world, where powerful changes could happen.

My journey into energy healing began out of curiosity about the unseen aspects of life. As I explored different healing methods, I discovered that ancient cultures didn't just recognize this energy—they lived in harmony with it. They built sacred sites in places of strong energy and celebrated the flow of cosmic energies in their daily lives.

Energy healing is more than just a physical cure; it offers a deeper understanding of ourselves and a connection to the universe. The energies around us can guide us, reveal truths, and help us live in harmony.

In our modern world, it's easy to question the relevance of ancient practices like energy healing. While technology and medicine are incredibly important, energy healing adds a holistic touch, supporting the body, mind, and spirit together.

This book aims to connect ancient wisdom with modern knowledge, presenting the timeless principles of energy healing in a way that resonates today. I will share my personal experiences, insights, and practices that have enriched my journey and may help you on yours.

Stay open and curious. Whether you're new to energy healing or already familiar with it, this journey offers a chance for deeper understanding and transformation.

Join me in this exploration of discovery and profound healing.

Warm regards,
Tom

Through the Eyes of an Energy Healer

CHAPTER I:
A JOURNEY OF DISCOVERY

My journey began in one of the western suburbs of Chicago, a place that, while comforting in its familiarity, felt like the starting point of a much larger adventure. My childhood and adolescence unfolded in that setting, but at the age of fifteen, I embarked on a journey that would profoundly shape my understanding of life and spirituality.

The decision to leave was impulsive, born out of frustration and a desire for something different. Without a clear plan or much money to my name, I set out for California to visit someone I knew who had relocated there. My brother had given me $35 for car expenses, a sum that seemed woefully inadequate for the trip ahead, but it was all I had. I remember feeling a mix of excitement and trepidation as I set off, with my faithful dog by my side. The open road symbolized freedom and the unknown, a stark contrast to the structured life I had always known.

The journey was anything but straightforward. Along the way, I found myself stopping at gas stations, looking for any work that could help me afford the next leg of the trip. One memorable instance involved a water pump replacement. I had never done such a task before, but with a sense of determination, I took on the challenge and successfully completed it. These small victories, born of necessity, taught me about resilience and resourcefulness in ways I hadn't anticipated. Each task, no matter how minor, reinforced my belief in my ability to overcome obstacles.

During this journey, I faced numerous challenges, including periods when I had to rely on the kindness of strangers. I stayed with the people I had gone to visit in California for over three weeks, an experience that was both humbling and eye-opening. Their generosity and warmth provided not only shelter but also a sense of community and belonging that I had longed for. I navigated the journey back to the Chicago area with a sense of accomplishment and a deeper appreciation for the kindness of others, realizing that human connections are a vital part of our spiritual and emotional well-being.

One particularly intense moment on this journey occurred while driving through the mountains on I-94. It was snowing heavily, and suddenly, my car began to spin uncontrollably. In that moment of panic, I clutched a cross given to me by my girlfriend and prayed for guidance and safety. It was a profound experience, one that underscored my belief in a higher power, even though I didn't adhere strictly to any religious doctrine. The howling wind and swirling snow seemed to mirror the turmoil within me, yet amidst the chaos, a sense of calm and protection enveloped me. It was an instance where spirit felt palpably present, guiding me through a potentially life-threatening situation.

Looking back, I see that this journey was more than a physical relocation; it was a quest for understanding and connection. Throughout my life, I struggled with intense empathic sensitivity, which often felt overwhelming. During my teenage years, I grappled with suicidal thoughts and found temporary solace in drugs and alcohol. These substances provided a brief escape from the emotional turmoil, but they were fleeting and ultimately unsustainable solutions. The emptiness I felt during those times was a stark reminder of the deeper issues I needed to address.

It wasn't until later in life that I encountered someone with psychic abilities who helped me understand my experiences more deeply. This individual explained that my profound sensitivity was a result of absorbing and living through the energies of others. This revelation was transformative, offering a framework to comprehend the emotional challenges I had faced. I began to recognize that my struggles were not merely personal failings but were connected to my heightened empathic abilities. Embracing this understanding allowed me to develop strategies to manage my sensitivity and harness it as a strength rather than a burden.

In the years that followed, I continued to travel extensively, seeking refuge and understanding in new places. My travels took me to various states, each offering unique experiences and insights. The constant movement was both a physical and emotional escape, allowing me to explore different facets of myself and the world around me. Through these experiences, I gradually discovered that the external journeys I undertook were reflections of an internal quest for healing and self-discovery. Every new location brought new lessons, friendships, and moments of introspection that contributed to my growth as an individual.

My travels and life experiences have ultimately led me to a profound realization: that the essence of our existence is deeply intertwined with the energies we encounter and the spiritual guidance we receive. The journey of self-discovery is not just about finding one's path but also about understanding the spiritual forces that shape and support us along the way. This chapter marks the beginning of that understanding, setting the stage for deeper explorations into the world of energy healing and the interconnectedness of all things.

CHAPTER 2:
THE POWER OF CHANNELING AND SELF-LOVE

From an early age, I discovered that I possessed a unique ability: the art of manipulation. It was a survival mechanism, one that I honed to navigate various situations and achieve my goals. This talent for influencing others became a significant part of my life, and I became adept at reading people and saying the right things to control outcomes. Over time, this skill served me well in many contexts, including my years working in repossession—a field where understanding and managing people's reactions was crucial.

In the realm of repossession, I had to use my abilities to ensure safety and manage delicate situations. Whether it was finding the right words to calm a distressed person or handling tense encounters with empathy, my knack for communication was put to the test. I learned that while we might think we have control over situations, true control often eludes us. Instead, navigating these moments with grace and understanding allowed me to manage outcomes effectively. This experience taught me the importance of emotional intelligence and the profound impact of compassionate interaction, reinforcing that true influence stems from genuine empathy rather than mere manipulation.

As my journey continued, spirit guided me towards a new purpose: helping people rather than manipulating them. The transition was profound. My creative outlets, which had once been focused on inventions and unique projects like building a life-size rickshaw in eighth grade, began to shift. I realized that being true to oneself and pursuing one's passions was essential, even if it meant standing out from the crowd or facing skepticism. This shift marked a pivotal moment in my life, where I began to prioritize authenticity and self-expression over strategic manipulation, paving the way for deeper personal growth and meaningful connections.

Society often pressures us to conform, but it's crucial to follow our own path and stay true to our unique gifts. Just as some individuals, despite numerous rejections, have persevered in their pursuits and achieved success, we too must trust in our journey. The path to fulfillment is deeply personal, and most of the people we encounter along the way are fleeting, their influence less significant than we might initially believe. Embracing this understanding allows us to focus on what truly matters, fostering a sense of inner peace and resilience against external pressures.

In the process of healing, I've learned that the most transformative moments often come from within. When clients come to me for healing, they frequently express a desire to help others. My response is simple: to truly help others, one must first practice self-love and compassion. It's essential to avoid judging others or letting their actions dictate our emotions. We never know the full extent of someone's struggles or the reasons behind their behavior. Instead of reacting with frustration or judgment, it's more beneficial to approach others with kindness and empathy. This inward focus not only enhances our ability to assist others but also cultivates a healthier, more balanced emotional state for ourselves.

The media often exacerbates this problem by focusing on fear and negativity, transforming hopeful stories into sensationalized horrors. This constant barrage of fear-based narratives can distort our perception of reality, making us feel as though we are living in a more dangerous world than we are. It's crucial to maintain a sense of perspective and not let these external influences dictate our internal state of being. Developing a mindful awareness of media consumption and actively seeking positive narratives can help preserve our mental and emotional well-being, allowing us to stay grounded amidst the chaos.

Creating spaces of comfort and sanctuary has become a central focus of my work. Whether through establishing welcoming environments in restaurants or other ventures, my goal has always been to provide a refuge where people can find solace and relaxation. A home or space should be a sanctuary, free from negative energies and conflicts. By regularly clearing negative energies and fostering a positive atmosphere, we can create environments that support well-being and healing. This dedication to creating harmonious spaces not only benefits those who enter them but also reinforces my commitment to promoting peace and positivity in every aspect of life.

In a world where quick fixes and pharmaceutical solutions often overshadow genuine healing, it's important to remember that true healing comes from within. The focus should be on addressing root causes rather than just treating symptoms. Self-love is at the heart of this process. When we love ourselves, we create a foundation for a more authentic and fulfilling life. This self-love extends to how we interact with others, shaping our ability to make a positive impact on their lives. By prioritizing inner healing and self-compassion, we lay the groundwork for lasting change and meaningful relationships.

Healing is about more than just addressing physical ailments—it's about nurturing the spirit and fostering genuine connections. Every act of kindness, every word of encouragement, has the potential to change lives. My journey has taught me that despite having many roles and experiences, the essence of healing lies in the simple act of being present, loving oneself, and extending that love to others. Embracing this holistic approach to healing not only transforms our own lives but also creates a ripple effect, inspiring others to cultivate love and compassion in their own journeys.

CHAPTER 3:
THE MODERN-DAY RESURGENCE

Standing at the crossroads of ancient practices and modern living, I'm amazed by the renewed interest in energy work. This resurgence isn't merely about revisiting old traditions but is a profound response to our fast-paced, technology-driven lives. Amidst the relentless rush and constant change, there seems to be a collective yearning to reconnect with something deeper—a form of healing that transcends the physical realm and addresses the entirety of our being.

Energy healing, which once seemed like an obscure practice relegated to the fringes of alternative medicine, is now gaining widespread acceptance. It's no longer confined to mystics and spiritual seekers alone. Today, energy work is being actively discussed in medical conferences, integrated into comprehensive wellness programs, and even featured in corporate wellness initiatives. This significant shift from being a niche interest to becoming part of mainstream conversation marks a transformative change in how we perceive health and well-being.

So why is energy work experiencing such a surge in popularity now? One compelling reason is the limitations inherent in our current medical practices. Modern medicine excels at addressing immediate health issues and managing symptoms with precision. However, it often overlooks the broader picture of human health—the intricate connection between mind, body, and spirit. As our understanding of health evolves, we're increasingly aware of this gap and are actively seeking ways to bridge it.

Energy work offers a holistic perspective, treating individuals as interconnected systems of energy rather than isolated physical entities. This approach resonates with those who believe that true healing involves more than just alleviating physical ailments. It encompasses the effects of emotions, thoughts, and the subtle energies that influence our overall well-being. By addressing these multifaceted aspects, energy work provides a more comprehensive pathway to health.

This modern resurgence in energy work feels like a collective awakening. It's an acknowledgment that we are inherently energetic beings and that this aspect plays a crucial role in our health and happiness. This understanding mirrors the beliefs of ancient cultures, which seamlessly integrated energy practices into their daily lives. The revival of these practices signifies a return to foundational truths about human existence and well-being.

I've observed people from all walks of life—scientists, healthcare professionals, artists, and everyday individuals—developing an interest in energy healing. This diverse mix of backgrounds underscores a shared recognition that there's more to our existence than the material world. It also highlights that the scientific community is beginning to explore these subtle aspects of our reality. Advances in quantum physics and studies of consciousness are gradually aligning with the principles of energy healing, creating a bridge between ancient wisdom and modern science.

Energy work's relevance today is further amplified by its inclusive approach to well-being. It complements modern medicine by addressing emotional and spiritual dimensions that traditional healthcare often overlooks. For instance, stress is a pervasive issue affecting many aspects of health. Energy healing practices such as Reiki, acupuncture, breathwork, and mindfulness specifically target the energetic roots of stress, offering relief that goes beyond mere symptom management.

In addition to enhancing physical health, energy work fulfills our deep-seated need for connection and purpose. In a world where we're constantly connected yet frequently feel isolated, practices like meditation do more than just help us relax—they enable us to explore our inner selves and establish a connection with something greater. This dual benefit addresses both our mental well-being and our spiritual needs, fostering a sense of belonging and purpose.

There's also a growing awareness that a purely

materialistic view of the world doesn't provide answers to all of life's profound questions. Energy work offers a pathway to touch the sacred, providing a perspective that extends beyond what is measurable and tangible. It invites us to consider the unseen forces that shape our lives and to honor the spiritual dimensions of our existence.

Many people are turning to energy work to reconnect with ancient wisdom. Practices like yoga, Tai Chi, and Qigong, which are grounded in age-old energy principles, are now recognized not just as physical exercises but as holistic methods for maintaining health and achieving balance. These practices exemplify how ancient techniques can be seamlessly integrated into modern lifestyles, enhancing both physical and spiritual well-being.

I've found that energy work is remarkably adaptable. It doesn't necessitate abandoning modern life but rather involves blending ancient wisdom with our daily routines. This synthesis creates a harmonious balance between tradition and progress, allowing us to benefit from the best of both worlds. By incorporating energy practices into our lives, we can navigate the complexities of modern existence with greater ease and resilience.

As we face the myriad challenges of contemporary life, energy work serves as a reminder of our interconnectedness and our innate ability to heal. It encourages individuals to take an active role in their health, fostering self-awareness and personal empowerment. Energy work acknowledges that healing is a multifaceted process, involving numerous dimensions with energy being a vital component of this intricate interplay of life.

In essence, the modern-day resurgence of energy work signifies a broader shift towards holistic health and a deeper understanding of our true nature. It bridges the gap between ancient traditions and contemporary needs, offering a comprehensive approach to well-being that honors both our physical and spiritual selves. This revival not only enhances our individual lives but also contributes to a collective movement towards a more balanced and harmonious world.

Through the Eyes of an Energy Healer

CHAPTER 4:
THE REALM OF ENERGY

To truly understand energy work, we need to grasp the concept of energy itself. Energy isn't just a buzzword or a scientific term—it's the very essence of everything around us. It's the invisible force that propels particles to move and shapes the vast expanse of the universe, from the smallest atoms to the grandest galaxies. This fundamental energy connects us all, influencing every facet of our lives in ways we are only beginning to comprehend.

Energy can be thought of as a universal currency. It flows through everything, not just through the electricity that powers our homes or the batteries in our devices. It permeates all aspects of existence, from the tiniest vibrations we can't see to the massive movements of galaxies. Nikola Tesla once said that to understand the universe, we should think in terms of energy, frequency, and vibration because everything is made of energy. For example, even though a table seems solid, it's actually composed of molecules that are in constant motion, vibrating at frequencies that sustain its structure, even if we can't perceive this movement with our senses.

In energy healing, this universal energy is considered the core of life. Different cultures have various names for this life force—prana in Indian traditions, chi in Chinese practices, or ki in Japanese beliefs—but they all agree that it's crucial for life and health. When this energy becomes unbalanced, it can cause disruptions in our physical health, emotions, or spiritual well-being, much like a blockage in a river can disrupt its flow and affect everything downstream. Understanding these imbalances is key to restoring harmony and promoting overall wellness.

Through my experience in energy healing, I've learned that this life force is omnipresent. It's present in both sacred places and ordinary settings, permeating every environment we inhabit. We live in a sea of energy, and our thoughts and feelings create waves in this vast field. This constant interplay of energy influences our interactions, our moods, and our physical health, highlighting the profound impact that subtle energies have on our daily lives.

Our bodies house intricate networks of energy pathways, known in different traditions as meridians or chakras. These pathways facilitate the smooth flow of energy, maintaining balance and promoting health. When this flow is interrupted by stress, trauma, or negative thoughts, it can lead to various health issues and emotional disturbances. Recognizing and addressing these blockages is essential for restoring vitality and ensuring our well-being.

Energy healing employs a variety of techniques to restore this vital flow. Methods like Reiki, acupuncture, breathwork, and qigong all acknowledge the presence of energy and utilize different approaches to work with it for healing purposes. Each technique offers unique ways to balance and harmonize the energy within and around us, contributing to a holistic approach to health.

Understanding that energy is everywhere isn't just a spiritual concept—it's increasingly supported by modern science, especially advancements in quantum physics. Research in areas like psychoneuroimmunology is beginning to demonstrate how our thoughts and emotions can significantly impact our physical health, linking the mind, body, and energy in a tangible way. These scientific insights are bridging the gap between ancient wisdom and contemporary understanding, validating the principles of energy healing through empirical evidence.

In everyday life, the effects of our energetic state might not always be immediately obvious, but they are undeniably powerful. The energy we project, influenced by our thoughts and feelings, can be sensed by those around us. When you enter a room filled with tension or happiness, you're not just experiencing a mood; you're tapping into the collective energy shaped by everyone's emotions and thoughts. This dynamic interaction underscores the importance of maintaining a positive and balanced energy state for both personal well-being and harmonious relationships.

This heightened awareness changes how we interact with the world. Our personal energy doesn't remain confined within us; it extends outward, influencing the spaces we occupy and the people we encounter. This interconnectedness reveals that we are part of a larger, dynamic energy field, where each individual contributes to the collective energy landscape. Recognizing this interdependence fosters a deeper sense of responsibility and mindfulness in how we manage our own energy and interact with others.

Energy healing is not merely a method of treatment—it's a way of perceiving and engaging with the world. It encourages us to actively participate in the flow of energy around us, rather than passively receiving care. This proactive stance highlights how our choices, thoughts, and feelings play a crucial role in shaping our health and experiences. By becoming more attuned to our own energy and that of others, we can cultivate a more balanced and harmonious existence.

The realm of energy healing reveals our profound connection with the universe. Our energies blend seamlessly with those of the earth, stars, and all living beings, creating a tapestry of interconnectedness that is both intricate and beautiful. This connection is not merely a philosophical idea but a practical reality that can guide us in various aspects of life, including health, relationships, and personal growth. By tuning into the subtle rhythms of the universe and aligning ourselves with its natural flow, we can tap into a powerful source of healing and transformation.

Embracing the realm of energy opens up a world of possibilities. It's about discovering how to work with the subtle forces that shape our lives, finding balance, and achieving harmony. Through practices like meditation, mindfulness, and various healing techniques, we can deepen our understanding of ourselves and our place in the universe. This journey into the realm of energy is not just about healing the body but also about nurturing the spirit and fostering a deeper connection with the world around us.

Through the Eyes of an Energy Healer

Chapter 5:
Everything Is Energy

The idea that everything is energy is the foundation of my exploration into energy healing. It marks a significant shift in how we understand reality, connecting the physical world with the more subtle, less visible aspects of existence. This concept transcends mystical ideas and reveals a fundamental truth about how everything in our universe operates and interacts.

Think about the ordinary objects around you—the chair you're sitting on, the phone you're holding, or even the words you're reading. At first glance, these things seem solid and unchanging. However, if you look closer through the lens of quantum physics, you'll see something entirely different. The particles that make up these objects are in a constant state of motion and vibration. These particles aren't solid; they are forms of energy in perpetual motion, vibrating at specific frequencies that give them their apparent solidity and form.

The idea that everything is energy isn't new or unique to modern science. Ancient cultures around the world have understood this for millennia. For example, Vedic texts describe the physical world as "maya," or an illusion that conceals the true energetic nature behind it. Various indigenous and spiritual traditions have also perceived the material world as a reflection of spiritual energy, recognizing that what we see is merely a surface layer of a deeper, energetic reality.

Understanding that everything is energy fundamentally changes how we view the world. It extends beyond just physical objects to encompass our thoughts and emotions. Emotions, which may seem fleeting and intangible, are actually powerful energy vibrations that impact our entire being. Our thoughts are not just abstract ideas; they are energy patterns that shape our reality. Positive thoughts can elevate our mood and foster well-being, while negative thoughts can create feelings of despair and discomfort. In this energetic universe, our thoughts and emotions play a crucial role in shaping our lives and experiences.

This perspective breaks down the old separation between the physical and metaphysical worlds. It suggests that the boundaries between ourselves and the world around us are not as solid as we might think. We are not merely passive observers of the universe but active participants in its energy flow, each contributing our unique energy to the grand cosmic dance. This interconnectedness implies that our individual energies are part of a larger, dynamic system that influences and is influenced by everything around us.

In terms of healing and personal growth, this perspective is revolutionary. It transforms how we approach health and wellness by suggesting that health problems are not solely physical issues but can also stem from disruptions in our energy fields. Just as the surface of a pond reflects what is happening beneath, our physical symptoms often indicate deeper energy imbalances. Recognizing these imbalances allows us to address the root causes of our ailments rather than merely treating the symptoms.

Energy healing practices aim to rectify these deeper disruptions by focusing on restoring balance and flow within our energy systems. Techniques such as Reiki, acupuncture, breathwork, and qigong all recognize the presence of energy and employ different methods to work with it for healing purposes. These practices focus on clearing blockages, removing stagnant energy, and reinstating the natural flow and balance of our life force, thereby promoting healing on physical, emotional, and spiritual levels. This holistic approach does not replace traditional medicine but complements it, offering a broader and more integrated pathway to health.

As I delved deeper into this new way of thinking, I initially struggled to let go of the belief that only what we can see and measure is real. However, witnessing the profound effects of energy healing in my own life and in the lives of others expanded my understanding. I realized that energetic blockages caused by stress, trauma, or negative thinking could lead to significant physical and emotional issues, underscoring the importance of maintaining a balanced energy flow for overall well-being.

Consider how energy healing operates: while traditional medicine might focus on alleviating symptoms, energy healing seeks to address the underlying causes of problems. This involves clearing blockages, removing stagnant energy, and restoring the natural flow and balance of our life force. By doing so, energy healing promotes a more profound and lasting sense of health and harmony.

The concept of energy being interconnected also transforms our view of groups and communities. Our individual energy contributes to a larger whole, with each thought, feeling, and action adding its own part to the collective energy. Shared experiences, such as moments of joy or sadness, illustrate how our energies intermingle and create a collective effect. This interconnectedness emphasizes the importance of cultivating positive energy not only for our own well-being but also for the benefit of those around us.

This interconnectedness of energy challenges the simplistic cause-and-effect thinking, demonstrating how our energy not only reflects but also influences and attracts experiences. Just like a tuning fork resonates with certain frequencies, our energy can align with and attract similar energies, shaping our life path and experiences. This understanding empowers us to consciously cultivate our energy to attract positive outcomes and foster a more fulfilling life.

This realization grants us immense power. It highlights our role in creating our own reality through our energy, emphasizing that we have the ability to influence our thoughts, emotions, and life direction. By understanding and utilizing the language of energy, we can take control of our personal and collective experiences, fostering a life of intention and purpose.

Accepting that everything is energy opens us up to a more expansive view of reality. This understanding serves as a powerful tool for personal and collective growth, helping us perceive ourselves and our world with greater clarity, compassion, and connection. As we continue to explore energy healing, we recognize that we are engaging with a vibrant, dynamic field of energy that connects and sustains all of existence, guiding us towards a more harmonious and enlightened way of living.

Through the Eyes of an Energy Healer

CHAPTER 6:
THE VIBRATIONAL NATURE OF EVERYTHING

When we dive into energy healing, one thing becomes clear: everything around us is full of vibrations. This idea isn't just a poetic way to describe the world—it's a fundamental truth that helps us understand how everything works, from the smallest particles to the largest galaxies. Recognizing the vibrational nature of all things provides a deeper insight into the interconnectedness of the universe and our place within it.

Think of the universe as a grand symphony, where everything is like a musical note. Every particle, every object, from the tiniest bits to the biggest stars, is part of this cosmic harmony. This idea harmonizes both ancient wisdom and modern science. Ancient philosophers and mystics understood that the universe is a dance of vibrations. For example, in Vedic traditions, there's the concept of "Om," a sacred sound that represents the essence of the universe. Many spiritual traditions have long believed that the physical world is just a manifestation of deeper vibrational energy, recognizing that what we perceive is a surface layer of a much more dynamic and energetic reality.

Modern science, especially quantum mechanics, supports this ancient knowledge. It reveals that subatomic particles are always vibrating, which challenges the old view of matter as solid and unchanging. This constant movement blurs the lines between matter and energy, unveiling a universe that is perpetually in flux. Quantum physics shows us that particles exist in a state of probability until they are observed, indicating that energy and vibration play crucial roles in the very fabric of reality.

To understand this better, think about a musical instrument. When a string on a guitar vibrates, it creates a sound. Similarly, the particles in the universe vibrate at different frequencies to make up the various forms of matter and energy we see. This cosmic melody is a complex mix of frequencies, with each element, from the tiniest particle to the largest star, playing its part in maintaining the balance and harmony of the universe.

As I explore this idea, I realize that everything has its own unique vibrational signature. This includes not just stars and galaxies but also our own planet. Earth has a natural vibration called the Schumann Resonance, which matches up with our brainwaves. This connection hints at a deep bond between us, the Earth, and the wider universe, suggesting that our well-being is closely tied to the vibrational state of our environment.

This concept of vibration is crucial in energy healing. It helps us understand how transformation and healing happen. In this view, health is about maintaining the right balance of vibrations in the body. When something is off, it can cause illness or discomfort. Energy healing practices, like sound therapy and Reiki, work to restore this balance by adjusting our vibrational frequencies to ones that support health and well-being. These practices recognize that the body is not just a physical entity but a dynamic field of energy that interacts with our thoughts, emotions, and spiritual state.

These practices see the body not just as a physical system but as a dynamic field of energy that interacts with our thoughts, emotions, and spiritual state. My own experiences with meditation and mindfulness have taught me that our thoughts and feelings have their own vibrations. This means they can influence the energy within us and around us. By tuning into these vibrations, we can guide ourselves toward better health and harmony, creating a more balanced and fulfilling life.

Our consciousness also plays a big role in this vibrational universe. Our thoughts and intentions send out vibrations that interact with the energy field described by quantum physics. By focusing on higher vibrational states like love, compassion, and gratitude, we can actively shape our reality. This intentional alignment with positive energies not only enhances our personal well-being but also contributes to the collective energy of our communities and the world at large.

The principle of resonance is a key part of this idea. Just like a tuning fork can make another tuning fork vibrate if they are the same frequency, our energy attracts and is attracted to similar vibrations. This idea, often called the law of attraction, suggests that the energy we put out through our thoughts and feelings draws experiences and situations that match our vibrational state. Understanding resonance empowers us to consciously cultivate our energy, fostering positive outcomes and nurturing a harmonious existence.

Understanding the vibrational nature of everything is both empowering and humbling. It shows us that we play an active role in creating our reality through the vibrations we choose to embody. Our inner state is not isolated but contributes to the collective energy that shapes our interactions with the world and the people around us. This awareness encourages us to take responsibility for our energy, promoting a more mindful and intentional approach to life.

In the grand scheme of the universe, this vibrational perspective changes how we see our existence. We are not just passive observers but active participants in the cosmic dance. Our choices, thoughts, and actions are like ripples in the vast sea of cosmic energy, each influencing the flow and balance of the universe. This interconnectedness highlights the importance of maintaining a positive and balanced vibrational state, not only for our own well-being but also for the harmony of the world around us.

This view also helps us approach life's challenges in a new way. By aligning our personal vibrations with positive frequencies, we can handle difficulties with greater ease and clarity. This doesn't mean ignoring problems but recognizing that our vibrational state can influence how we experience and overcome them. By maintaining a high vibrational frequency, we can navigate life's ups and downs with resilience and grace, fostering a sense of peace and empowerment.

The vibrational nature of everything also underscores the interconnectedness of all life. Our actions and states of being affect not just ourselves but the larger world around us. By fostering positive vibrations within ourselves, we contribute to the collective energy and impact the world in meaningful ways. This interconnectedness calls us to cultivate harmony and positivity, enhancing not only our own lives but also the lives of those we interact with.

In personal growth and development, understanding vibrations opens up new possibilities. It encourages us to seek harmony in both our inner and outer worlds, guiding us toward practices that support our physical, emotional, and spiritual well-being. This journey is about more than just individual healing; it's about contributing to the overall harmony of the world. By embracing the vibrational nature of everything, we unlock our potential for transformation and create a more balanced and harmonious existence.

As we explore the vibrational nature of everything, we step into a realm where energy and consciousness are intertwined. We discover that the universe is like a grand symphony, and we each have a unique role to play in its rhythm. By understanding and embracing this vibrational nature, we unlock our potential and find a path to transformation, leading us toward a more enlightened and harmonious way of living.

Chapter 7:
The Weaving of the Physical and Spiritual

In our lives, the connection between our physical and spiritual energies is a fundamental part of who we are. It's like a graceful dance that intertwines these two aspects of ourselves, shaping our entire experience in profound and intricate ways. This relationship is not merely an abstract idea but a tangible reality that affects every part of our being, influencing our health, emotions, and overall sense of purpose.

Our physical body is an amazing creation, a vessel through which we interact with the world, experiencing life through our senses. It allows us to touch, see, hear, taste, and smell, providing a direct connection to our environment. But inside this physical form lies something deeper: our spiritual energy. This energy transcends the physical realm, offering us a glimpse into the more profound and intangible aspects of our existence. It is the essence that gives life its vibrancy and meaning, bridging the gap between the material and the metaphysical.

Understanding that our body and spirit are intrinsically linked is crucial to truly knowing who we are. The body is not just a collection of cells and organs; it is the physical manifestation of our life force, energized and sustained by our spiritual essence. This profound connection is evident in how our physical state can significantly impact our spiritual experiences and vice versa. When our body is healthy and vibrant, our spirit feels uplifted and inspired, enhancing our overall well-being.

Ancient wisdom has long respected the body as a sacred place for the spirit, likening it to a temple for our soul. This reverence encourages us to take meticulous care of our bodies, recognizing that maintaining physical health is intrinsically linked to supporting our spiritual well-being. Practices such as proper nutrition, regular exercise, and mindful living are not just about physical fitness but also about honoring the spiritual energy that resides within us.

The connection between body and spirit is vividly evident in practices that engage both, such as yoga or mindful walking in nature. These activities are not merely physical exercises; they are holistic practices designed to bring our physical and spiritual selves into harmonious alignment. Through intentional movement and focused breathing, we create a bridge that unites our bodily sensations with our inner consciousness, fostering a deep sense of balance and peace. Even something as simple as conscious breathing can connect us profoundly with our inner selves, calming the mind and rejuvenating the spirit.

Our emotions further illustrate how the physical and spiritual aspects of ourselves are interconnected. Positive emotions like joy, love, and gratitude elevate our spiritual vibration and enhance our physical health, creating a harmonious state of being. Conversely, physical pain or illness often reflects underlying issues in our spiritual or emotional state, highlighting the close relationship between our body and soul. This interplay suggests that emotional well-being is just as important as physical health in maintaining overall harmony.

Energy healing practices are centered around this vital connection. Methods such as Reiki, acupuncture, and chakra balancing operate on the principle that physical problems can stem from blockages or imbalances in our energy fields. These practices aim to restore balance by addressing both the physical symptoms and their deeper energetic causes. By harmonizing our energy systems, energy healing facilitates healing on multiple levels—physical, emotional, and spiritual—promoting a comprehensive sense of well-being.

Sometimes, the barrier between the physical and spiritual worlds seems to fade, allowing us to experience a sense of unity and oneness. These moments—whether they occur in the serenity of nature, through the creation of art, or within our meaningful relationships—serve as powerful reminders of the seamless blend between our physical and spiritual lives. They highlight the interconnectedness of all aspects of our existence, reinforcing the idea that our physical and spiritual selves are not separate entities but integral parts of a unified whole.

Our consciousness plays a pivotal role in connecting the physical and spiritual realms. Our thoughts, beliefs, and perceptions act as a bridge between the tangible and intangible parts of our lives. By changing our consciousness, we can transform our experiences, allowing us to perceive our physical reality through a spiritual lens. This shift in perspective enables us to approach life with greater awareness and intentionality, fostering a deeper connection with our true selves.

In this context, the idea of alignment takes on a profound meaning. True alignment occurs when our physical bodies are healthy and our spiritual energies are flowing smoothly. This state of harmony is not static but requires ongoing attention and mindfulness. It involves actively listening to and responding to the needs of both our body and spirit, ensuring that neither is neglected. Achieving and maintaining this balance is a dynamic process, involving continuous self-reflection and adaptation.

As we explore the connection between our physical and spiritual selves, we tap into the innate wisdom within us. Our body, with its natural intelligence, communicates through sensations and intuition, guiding us toward what it needs for optimal health. Our spirit, a source of boundless energy and consciousness, seeks to express itself and grow through our physical experiences. This dialogue between body and spirit fosters a deeper understanding of ourselves, enabling us to nurture both aspects harmoniously.

By embracing the relationship between the physical and spiritual, we gain a holistic understanding of our existence. We become active participants in our own well-being, recognizing that true health involves the integration of our physical, emotional, and spiritual dimensions. This journey is about more than just individual healing; it's about discovering ourselves more deeply and exploring the endless possibilities that arise when we honor and nurture the balance between our tangible and intangible aspects. Through this integrated approach, we unlock our potential for profound personal growth and a more fulfilling, harmonious life.

Through the Eyes of an Energy Healer

Chapter 8:
Deciphering the Body's Silent Language

Our physical body is more than just a collection of organs and tissues; it's a sensitive and responsive system that picks up on the subtle energies around us. This means our bodies are constantly translating and reacting to the energetic environment we live in. This process is a silent yet profound dialogue between our physical presence and the invisible energies that affect us, creating a continuous interplay that influences our overall well-being.

Our bodies react to the flow of energy in numerous ways. For instance, you might feel tingling or warmth when there's a change in your energetic surroundings. These sensations can be subtle, like a gentle warmth on your skin, or more noticeable, such as a tingling sensation running through your body. These responses often signal that something significant is happening in the energetic field around you, acting as early warning signs or indicators of shifts in your environment or internal state.

Breathing is another key indicator of our energetic state. When you take time to breathe deeply and mindfully, you can gauge how your internal energy is doing. A deep and steady breath often means you're feeling calm and centered, facilitating a harmonious flow of energy throughout your body. On the other hand, if your breath is rapid and shallow, it might be a sign that you're feeling stressed or agitated, disrupting the natural balance of your energy. Your breath mirrors the state of your inner energy, giving you invaluable clues about your emotional and spiritual condition, and serving as a tool for self-regulation and balance.

Emotions also have a profound physical impact on our bodies. For example, you might feel a sense of lightness and joy in your chest when you're happy or a heaviness in your stomach when you're sad or grieving. These physical sensations are not random; they're the body's way of expressing and processing what you're feeling emotionally. This intricate connection between emotions and physical sensations underscores the importance of addressing both emotional and physical health for overall harmony.

Our bodies also react to different environments in distinct ways. When you're in nature, where the energy is clean and refreshing, you might feel energized and at ease, experiencing a rejuvenating effect that revitalizes both body and spirit. Conversely, in crowded or energetically charged places, you might feel tight or uncomfortable, as your body responds to the heightened or conflicting energies in your surroundings. This sensitivity highlights the profound impact that our environment has on our energetic state, emphasizing the need to create and seek out spaces that support our well-being.

In practices like energy healing, physical sensations can indicate that energy is being released or realigned. For instance, during a Reiki session or meditation, you might experience warmth or tingling. These feelings are not just side effects; they are integral parts of the healing process, showing that energy pathways are being cleared and balanced. These sensations serve as tangible evidence that the energy work is facilitating a flow that promotes healing and restoration, bridging the gap between the physical and energetic aspects of health.

Sometimes, when you experience a deep spiritual insight or connection, you might get what people call "truth bumps" or "spiritual chills." These sensations happen when your body resonates with a profound truth or alignment, creating a physical response that mirrors your spiritual awakening. They are more than physical reactions; they confirm that you're in tune with a higher wisdom or energy, reinforcing the connection between your physical sensations and spiritual experiences.

However, our bodies also show us when there is energetic discord. For example, stress often results in physical symptoms like muscle tension, headaches, or fatigue. These signs are not just random discomforts; they indicate an imbalance in your energetic state, signaling that your body and spirit are out of sync. Recognizing and addressing these signs is crucial for restoring balance and health, allowing you to respond proactively to maintain your well-being.

By viewing the body as an interpreter of energy, we gain a deeper understanding of our experiences. Paying attention to physical responses is a way to connect more deeply with the energies around us, fostering a heightened awareness of how our bodies communicate with our environment. Listening to the body's silent language helps us navigate life with greater awareness and harmony, enabling us to respond to energetic cues with mindfulness and intention.

As we continue to explore this relationship, we learn to appreciate and interpret the body's signals as valuable guidance. Each sensation, change in breath, and physical reaction is a clue, helping us understand the complex interplay of energy in our lives. In this ongoing process, the body becomes a reliable guide, leading us to a richer connection with the energies that shape our existence and our place in the grand scheme of things. This enhanced awareness empowers us to take control of our health and well-being, using our bodies as powerful tools for deciphering and harmonizing the energies that influence every aspect of our lives.

Chapter 9:
The Emotional Gateway

Emotions are much more than fleeting feelings; they are powerful doors that offer deep insights into our lives, seamlessly linking the physical and spiritual worlds. Emotions paint our experiences with a wide range of feelings, each color revealing something unique and profound about our inner selves. They serve as indicators, guiding us through our personal journeys and highlighting areas that need attention and healing.

I've come to see emotions as wise messengers, providing us with glimpses into the core of our being. Each emotion, whether it's the gentle contentment of peace or the intense energy of passion, helps us understand our connection with the universe on a deeper level. They are not random or meaningless; instead, they carry messages that can lead us to greater self-awareness and spiritual growth.

Joy, for example, is more than just a moment of

happiness. It's a powerful force that lifts our spirits and fills us with wonder and gratitude. When we feel joy, it often manifests as a lightness in our body, a kind of glowing energy that touches every cell. This vibrant sensation acts as a bridge, connecting us to higher energies and allowing us to experience a sense of something greater than ourselves. Joy not only enhances our mood but also aligns us with positive vibrations that foster overall well-being and spiritual alignment.

On the other hand, sorrow and grief take us on a deeper journey into our emotions. These feelings can be heavy and overwhelming, but they also offer a chance for profound personal growth. The tears we shed during times of grief can cleanse us, breaking down emotional barriers and allowing us to connect more deeply with the spiritual side of life. In these moments of vulnerability, we often find a closer connection to universal truths that unite us all, fostering a sense of empathy and shared humanity.

Anger, while often seen as a negative emotion, can be a powerful force for change when we handle it wisely. This intense feeling can drive us to take meaningful action, whether it's fighting for justice or addressing wrongs in our lives. By channeling anger in a constructive way, we can find new purpose and direction, moving through both physical and spiritual realms with renewed energy and determination. Anger, when understood and managed, becomes a catalyst for transformation and positive change.

Fear, though sometimes viewed negatively, holds its

own wisdom. When approached with respect, fear can guide us by showing us where we need to be cautious or where we should explore more deeply. Fear acts as a protective force, helping us navigate the complexities of our experiences with greater awareness and care. It alerts us to potential dangers and encourages us to develop resilience and courage, ultimately strengthening our ability to face challenges with confidence.

Love is perhaps the most transformative of all emotions. It creates bonds that go beyond the physical, connecting us on a spiritual level. Acting from a place of love—through compassion, empathy, and connection— helps us tap into a universal energy that breaks down the illusion of separation and reveals our deep connection with everyone around us. Love nurtures our relationships, fosters unity, and promotes a sense of belonging and fulfillment, enhancing both our personal and collective well-being.

Emotions are not just personal experiences; they are integral parts of a collective human story. By engaging with our emotions mindfully, we become more aware of the ebb and flow of energy within and around us. This heightened awareness helps us navigate our personal journeys with greater clarity and purpose, while also connecting us to the broader human experience. Understanding and embracing our emotions allows us to participate more fully in the shared tapestry of life, fostering a sense of community and interconnectedness.

In times of strong emotions, whether joy or sorrow, there is an energetic shift within us. These emotions act like tuning forks, resonating with the unseen energies around us. Joy aligns us with higher spiritual vibrations, while sorrow connects us more deeply with our human experiences and the realities of life. This dynamic interaction highlights the profound impact that our emotional states have on our energetic balance and overall harmony.

Emotions are a shared language that connects us all. Observing how others express their emotions gives us insight into the collective human soul and the dynamic energies that shape our shared reality. This understanding fosters empathy and compassion, enabling us to relate to others on a deeper level and build stronger, more meaningful connections.

As I delve deeper into understanding emotions, I see them as gateways to greater insight. They help us unlock the mysteries of both the physical and spiritual worlds, guiding us through our experiences with wisdom and grace. By embracing our emotions, we engage in a sacred practice that allows us to explore both seen and unseen realms, guided by the innate wisdom of the heart. This journey through our emotions is about connection—it shows how deeply we are intertwined with each other and with the universe, reinforcing the idea that our emotional experiences are integral to our spiritual growth and understanding.

Recognizing the depth and power of our emotions opens us to a fuller understanding of our existence. Emotions teach us about resilience and vulnerability, demonstrating that acknowledging and expressing our feelings leads to growth, healing, and deeper spiritual connections. They reveal the strength in our ability to endure and the beauty in our capacity to love and empathize, shaping us into more compassionate and enlightened individuals.

Emotions are not passive; they actively shape how we see and interact with the world. How we respond to and express our emotions impacts our personal development and relationships. They influence our decisions, our connections with others, and our journey toward realizing our true selves. By embracing all our emotional experiences, we learn to navigate life with greater authenticity and bravery. Each emotion, whether challenging or joyful, is a crucial part of being human, contributing to our overall growth and understanding.

As we become more in tune with our emotions, we develop a deeper sense of empathy and compassion, both for ourselves and for others. We start to recognize the shared experiences of joy, sorrow, fear, and love that connect us all, fostering unity and understanding. This emotional gateway is a vital part of our journey, connecting us to both the physical and spiritual realms in ways that are uniquely meaningful to each of us. Through this deep emotional awareness, we cultivate a life of balance, harmony, and profound connection with the world around us.

CHAPTER 10:
THOUGHTS, FEELINGS, AND ENERGY

Our thoughts and feelings are crucial in shaping our lives. They weave together the energy that makes up our reality, creating a tapestry of experiences that define who we are and how we interact with the world around us. Over time, I've learned just how much our inner world—our thoughts and feelings—affects the energy around us, influencing not only our personal well-being but also the broader environment we inhabit.

I've come to realize that our thoughts are not just fleeting mental activities. They are vibrant pulses of energy that carry immense power. Each thought we have sends out a specific energy frequency into the world, acting like ripples in a vast pond. Whether we're aware of them or not, these thoughts affect our personal energy field and the energy around us, subtly shaping our interactions and experiences. This continuous flow of thoughts creates an energetic imprint that can attract similar energies, reinforcing the patterns we establish in our lives.

When we think positively, with feelings of love, gratitude, and optimism, we raise our energy level significantly. I've noticed that when I focus on positive thoughts, the atmosphere around me becomes lighter and clearer, almost as if a weight has been lifted. It's like tuning into a frequency where joy, peace, and harmony are stronger, creating an environment that nurtures growth and positivity. These elevated energy states not only enhance our mood but also attract more positive experiences, fostering a cycle of continual upliftment and well-being.

On the other hand, negative thoughts, often fueled by fear, doubt, or criticism, can disrupt our energy balance. These negative thoughts can make us feel heavy or uneasy, creating a sense of stagnation and discomfort. This imbalance not only affects how we feel inside but can also attract situations that mirror these lower energy levels, perpetuating a cycle of negativity and limitation. Recognizing and addressing these negative patterns is essential for restoring our energy balance and promoting a healthier, more harmonious existence.

Beliefs, the deeply held convictions that shape our view of ourselves and the world, have an even bigger impact on our energy. These beliefs, which come from our experiences and cultural influences, act as filters for how we see reality. They can either limit or expand our energy potential, determining the scope of our possibilities and the extent of our personal growth. Limiting beliefs, like those that make us feel unworthy or incapable, create barriers in our energy, making us feel trapped and preventing us from seeing all the possibilities available to us. It's like wearing blinders that restrict our vision, keeping us confined within self-imposed boundaries.

In contrast, empowering beliefs open us up to endless possibilities. When we hold beliefs that affirm our worth and our ability to grow, our energy transforms in profound ways. We break free from limitations and open ourselves to new opportunities and experiences that align with our higher energy state. These empowering beliefs act as catalysts for positive change, enhancing our resilience and capacity to navigate life's challenges with confidence and grace.

The interaction between our thoughts, feelings, and energy is like a creative dance, a harmonious interplay that shapes our reality. Our thoughts, filled with emotional energy, boost our vibrational frequency, setting the tone for our experiences. Our beliefs shape these vibrations and help them manifest in our physical reality, turning the unseen into the seen, and allowing what we imagine to take shape in our lives. This dynamic process underscores the profound impact that our inner world has on the outer world, highlighting the power we hold as creators of our own reality.

Awareness is key to mastering this dance. By paying attention to our thoughts and feelings, we can actively shape our energy reality, consciously directing our vibrational frequencies toward desired outcomes. Letting go of negative thoughts and beliefs helps us connect with higher energy levels, leading to growth and transformation. This mindful approach empowers us to take control of our emotional and energetic states, fostering a sense of agency and intentionality in our lives.

Similarly, nurturing positive beliefs and engaging in positive thinking can reshape our energy field in transformative ways. This inner work allows us to break free from limiting patterns and embrace a life full of greater potential and fulfillment. By cultivating empowering beliefs, we enhance our capacity to attract and create positive experiences, aligning our energy with our highest aspirations and deepest desires.

In energy work, our thoughts and beliefs are the threads that create our life's fabric. Each intentional thought and belief contributes to a vibrant and harmonious energy field, weaving together the intricate patterns of our existence. This blend of positive, loving, and abundant energies creates a resonance that extends beyond us, affecting the collective energy and helping to make the world more harmonious. By fostering positive energy within ourselves, we contribute to the overall vibrational harmony of our communities and the planet, promoting a sense of unity and collective well-being.

As we explore the relationship between thoughts, feelings, and energy, we learn to be conscious creators of our reality. We see how our inner world influences our outer world and recognize the deep connections between everything. This understanding helps us on our journey of self-discovery, guiding us to align our thoughts and feelings with our true intentions and aspirations. By embracing this powerful interplay, we unlock our potential to shape our lives with intention and purpose, fostering a harmonious and fulfilling existence.

In essence, our thoughts and feelings are not just passive experiences but active forces that shape our energy and, consequently, our reality. By harnessing the power of positive thinking and nurturing empowering beliefs, we can transform our lives and the world around us. This chapter highlights the profound impact of our inner world on our energetic and physical realities, encouraging us to cultivate a mindful and intentional approach to our thoughts and emotions. Through this conscious cultivation, we become architects of our own destinies, creating a life that reflects our highest potentials and deepest truths.

Through the Eyes of an Energy Healer

CHAPTER 11:
ENERGY MOVES AND WE WITH IT

Watching children dance to music, completely absorbed in the rhythm and unaware of the world around them, offers a beautiful example of how deeply we are connected to the energy that shapes our lives. These moments remind us of our natural bond with the vibrations flowing through the universe, a connection we often lose sight of as we grow older. The innocence and purity of children's dance highlight a fundamental truth about our existence and our intrinsic relationship with the energetic forces that surround us.

When children dance, they express themselves in a pure and unfiltered way. They aren't trying to impress anyone or fit in; instead, they react instinctively to the energy of the music. Their movements are a natural response to the vibrations they feel, embodying a seamless harmony between their physical actions and the surrounding energy. This spontaneous reaction underscores a key truth about who we are: we are beings of energy, inherently in tune with the rhythms and frequencies that permeate our environment. Music, in this context, acts as a powerful trigger, tapping into the energetic currents that many adults might overlook or suppress due to self-consciousness, societal expectations, or mental conditioning. This innate responsiveness to energy reveals the profound potential we have to reconnect with our true selves.

Children's uninhibited dancing demonstrates how aligning with these energetic frequencies can lead to a profound sense of freedom and authenticity. It's not merely about moving physically; it's about surrendering to the natural flow of energy that sustains us. This deep connection to music's vibrations uncovers a healing aspect that often gets lost in our structured adult lives, where routine and responsibility can stifle our ability to freely express and engage with our energetic selves. By observing children, we are reminded of the joy and liberation that comes from embracing our energetic nature without reservation.

Music's healing power extends far beyond just listening. It penetrates into the very core of our being, where the frequencies in music resonate with our deepest selves, stirring emotions and causing shifts in our energy fields. This potential for transformation is not limited to traditional melodies but encompasses all types of music that resonate with us personally. Each genre, rhythm, and beat can evoke different emotional and energetic responses, allowing for a diverse range of healing experiences tailored to individual needs. The versatility of music in energy healing showcases its universal applicability and profound impact on our well-being.

When people come together to dance to diverse or unconventional music, there is a powerful exchange of energy. At first, the scene might seem unusual, but as you immerse yourself in the experience, it becomes clear that everyone is interacting with frequencies that connect with them individually. The music becomes a unifying force, a shared language that is spoken through the movement of our bodies, transcending words and traditional norms. This collective engagement creates a vibrant energy field that enhances the overall experience, fostering a sense of community and shared purpose. The synergy generated in these moments highlights the collective nature of energy and the profound impact of shared vibrational experiences.

In these moments, music connects us to experiences beyond the everyday. It allows us to tap into dimensions of energy that we might not usually perceive, offering glimpses into the unseen layers of our existence. Music invites us to let go of mental constraints and let our bodies become channels for the free flow of energy, facilitating a state of flow where we are fully present and engaged. This can be a cathartic experience, providing a way to release pent-up emotions and connect with the unseen energies that guide the universe. The therapeutic benefits of such experiences underscore the importance of integrating music and movement into our lives as tools for emotional and energetic healing.

Seeing children's dance as a meaningful connection

with the universe's vibrational essence encourages us to rethink our own relationship with music and movement. It invites us to rediscover the joy and freedom of moving instinctively to the rhythms around us, embracing a form of expression that is both natural and deeply fulfilling. By reconnecting with this natural form of expression, we can harness the healing power of music, allowing it to uplift and transform us. This reconnection fosters a sense of authenticity and alignment with our true energetic nature, promoting overall well-being and spiritual growth.

Ultimately, dancing to music, whether as a child or an adult, is a return to a basic form of communication with the universe. It's a chance to remember a language we once knew—the language of energy and vibration—and let it guide us toward healing and connection. This rediscovery of our natural ability to move with the energy around us is a journey back to the essence of who we are, finding joy and simplicity in living harmoniously with the cosmic dance of life. Embracing this journey allows us to tap into our innate potential for transformation, fostering a life of balance, joy, and profound connection with the universe and those around us.

Chapter 12:
From Fear to Love

In our lives, we often move between two powerful feelings: fear and love. These emotions, though very different, shape our experiences and teach us important lessons. Love, with its bright and warm energy, helps us connect deeply with others. Fear, on the other hand, can be a challenge that we need to face as we grow and understand ourselves better. This dynamic interplay between fear and love is fundamental to our emotional and spiritual development, guiding us through the complexities of human experience.

Love is a special kind of energy that vibrates at a very high level. It shows up in many ways—like the warmth of a hug or the strong connections we have with people, no matter how far apart we are. This energy of love goes beyond just us as individuals. It taps into a universal source that brings us together and helps us live our lives to the fullest. Love invites us to enjoy the joy and harmony that is naturally a part of life, fostering a sense of belonging and unity. It acts as a powerful catalyst for creating meaningful relationships and nurturing a supportive community around us.

In our emotional world, love is like the thread that connects us all. It brings us closer together, helping us to be more empathetic, compassionate, and deeply connected with each other. Whether we show love to others or give it to ourselves through self-compassion, love forms the foundation for exploring our inner selves and appreciating the world around us. This self-love is crucial for our personal growth, as it enables us to accept ourselves fully and extend that acceptance to others, creating a ripple effect of positivity and understanding.

Fear, in contrast, comes from our basic instincts. It acts as a sort of guardian, warning us about dangers and helping us navigate uncertain situations. But when fear takes over, it can block our view and make it hard for us to fully enjoy life. Fear can create barriers, twist our understanding, and often lead us into confusion and insecurity. It can immobilize us, preventing us from taking necessary risks and embracing new opportunities. However, fear also serves as a vital signal, alerting us to potential threats and encouraging us to prepare and protect ourselves.

Moving from fear to love is not a quick or easy process. It involves a constant shift in how we see things, a willingness to face and understand our fears, and the bravery to let go of beliefs that hold us back. In this journey, love becomes a powerful force, changing the energy of fear into chances for growth, learning, and deeper connections. This transformation requires patience and persistence, as we work to reframe our fears and replace them with empowering beliefs that support our highest potential.

To embrace this change, we need to be aware of how fear and love interact. They are not fixed emotions but energies that change and flow within us. By learning to balance these emotions, we can experience fear without letting it control us and embrace love in all its forms. This balance allows us to respond to life's challenges with resilience and grace, maintaining our inner peace even in difficult times. Developing this awareness helps us cultivate emotional intelligence, enabling us to navigate our feelings with greater skill and understanding.

Love helps us navigate through our fears. It encourages us to open our hearts, be vulnerable, and find strength in being truly ourselves. As we grow more loving, we begin to see fear not as something to be feared but as a guide, helping us become more aware and compassionate. This shift in perspective allows us to transform fear into a tool for personal development, using it to uncover deeper truths about ourselves and our place in the world. By integrating love into our response to fear, we create a harmonious balance that enhances our overall well-being and spiritual growth.

The relationship between fear and love is an important part of being human. Both emotions have a role, giving us valuable insights into ourselves and our relationships. As we move through these feelings, we learn to appreciate the depth and richness of our emotional lives. This appreciation fosters a greater sense of empathy and connection with others, as we recognize that everyone experiences this emotional spectrum. Understanding the interplay between fear and love enriches our interactions, allowing us to support and uplift one another in meaningful ways.

We need to accept and understand both love and fear, knowing that each has a role in shaping who we are. By working with these emotions, we turn challenges into chances for growth. Standing at the crossroads of fear and love reminds us of the power of choosing love. This choice opens us up to a life full of meaning, joy, and connection. It empowers us to rise above our fears, embracing love as a guiding force that leads us toward a more fulfilling and harmonious existence.

May we explore our emotions with compassion and curiosity. May we find the courage to face our fears, learn from them, and open our hearts to the power of love. By doing so, we step into a more genuine, connected, and fulfilling life, creating a reality that celebrates the full range of our human experiences. Embracing this emotional journey allows us to transform fear into love, fostering a life of balance, resilience, and profound connection with ourselves and the world around us.

Chapter 13:
The Power of Negative and Positive Emotions

In the intricate dance of life, both positive and negative emotions wield significant influence over our experiences, shaping our spiritual and physical well-being. Understanding the energetic effects of these emotions provides profound insight into how they impact our lives and guide us on our journey toward self-discovery and fulfillment.

The concept of duality often arises in discussions about emotions and spiritual growth. Some believe in a strict balance, such as the idea that we must maintain a 50/50 split between light and dark. This perspective suggests that our spiritual development requires an equal measure of positive and negative experiences. However, my personal view diverges from this notion. I believe that while we are part of a collective experience, our individual balance doesn't need to adhere to a rigid formula. Instead, it's about the proportion of light and darkness that resonates with each person and how we evolve within that spectrum. This flexible approach acknowledges the uniqueness of each individual's emotional landscape, allowing for a more personalized path to spiritual and emotional harmony.

For instance, one might argue that if many people embody a significant amount of darkness, it's possible to strive for a higher ratio of light—perhaps 80% light and 20% darkness. This approach acknowledges that as we raise our vibration, we naturally diminish the presence of darkness in our lives. The goal isn't to eliminate negativity entirely but to shift the balance towards a more harmonious and elevated state of being. By fostering an environment where positive energies can thrive, we create space for growth, resilience, and a deeper connection to our true selves.

Our emotional landscape is rich and multifaceted, encompassing both positive and negative experiences. Positive emotions—such as love, joy, and gratitude—emit powerful vibrations that elevate our spirits and strengthen our connection to the universe. Love, in its purest form, radiates a harmonious energy that heals and unites us with the divine essence present in all things. When we experience love, our soul feels nurtured and aligned with a higher frequency, fostering deep spiritual connections that enhance our sense of purpose and belonging.

Joy, another uplifting emotion, brings lightness and happiness, expanding our energy field and attracting positive experiences into our lives. It serves as a reminder of our innate link to the universal source of happiness, opening us to more of life's wonderful moments. Embracing joy can transform our outlook and enhance our overall well-being, acting as a beacon that draws more positivity and abundance into our lives.

Gratitude, though gentle, is a potent force that invites abundance into our lives. Practicing gratitude tunes us into appreciation for what we have and makes us more receptive to receiving blessings. It helps us recognize the sacredness in everyday moments and imbues our journey with meaning. By cultivating gratitude, we align our energy with the flow of abundance, fostering a mindset that attracts prosperity and fulfillment.

Conversely, negative emotions such as fear, anger, and sadness play crucial roles in our emotional landscape, despite their challenges. Fear, once essential for survival, can hinder spiritual growth if it dominates our lives. It can block our energy and create distance from our spiritual self. However, when we face and understand our fears, they can become sources of strength and empowerment, guiding us through personal transformation. Fear challenges us to step out of our comfort zones, fostering courage and resilience that propel us toward greater self-awareness and spiritual depth.

Anger is a powerful emotion with the potential for both destruction and positive change. When channeled constructively, anger can drive us to address issues and build resilience. It compels us to assert ourselves and pursue actions that lead to meaningful outcomes.

Harnessing anger effectively requires self-awareness and intentionality, transforming it from a force of disruption into a catalyst for positive action and personal growth.

Sadness, often perceived as a negative feeling, can serve as a pathway to emotional and spiritual renewal. Much like rain nourishes the earth, sadness can cleanse our inner self, allowing new insights and perspectives to emerge. When processed healthily, sadness offers an opportunity for growth and deeper understanding. It encourages us to reflect, heal, and reconnect with our true selves, fostering a sense of empathy and compassion that enriches our relationships and spiritual journey.

Balancing positive and negative emotions is a skill that involves awareness and thoughtful engagement. Emotions act as messengers, providing clues about our inner state and guiding us toward equilibrium or highlighting areas that need attention. Embracing our emotional journey means recognizing that our feelings resonate with different energies, helping us navigate through life's complexities with greater insight and resilience.

In this symphony of emotions, both positive and negative experiences contribute to the richness of our lives. Our path to spiritual and physical well-being invites us to be mindful conductors of this emotional orchestra, finding harmony in our feelings and using them as tools for growth and healing. By integrating and balancing our emotional spectrum, we come to appreciate the depth and richness of our experiences, understanding that every emotion—whether luminous or shadowed—

enriches the unique masterpiece of our lives.

Ultimately, the power of negative and positive emotions lies in their ability to shape our reality and guide our spiritual evolution. By embracing both sides of our emotional spectrum, we cultivate a balanced and holistic approach to life, fostering a deeper connection with ourselves and the universe. This balanced emotional state not only enhances our personal well-being but also contributes to a more harmonious and compassionate world, where the full range of human experiences is valued and integrated into our collective journey.

Through the Eyes of an Energy Healer

Chapter 14:
And So Jealousy Comes Forward

Facing and overcoming jealousy is a significant chapter in my life. This emotion, often dark and damaging, had deeply influenced my actions and clouded my perspective. Looking back, I see how important it was for me to become aware of this emotion and how mastering it led to profound personal growth and transformation.

Jealousy, with its sneaky and harmful nature, had become a pervasive part of my life, affecting my relationships and interactions in subtle yet impactful ways. It manifested as a mix of anger and resentment, creating a relentless cycle of negativity that seemed impossible to break. What I didn't realize at the time was that these feelings were not entirely my own; they were influenced by external factors and energies that I had absorbed without conscious awareness, further complicating my emotional landscape.

A turning point came one night that made me see my

jealousy in a new light. I had an interaction that revealed just how deep my jealousy went and how it was affecting not only me but also those around me. Witnessing the impact of similar emotions in someone else's life was a harsh wake-up call. It made me understand that my jealousy was not just a personal struggle but had real consequences for my interactions with others, highlighting the importance of addressing these feelings for the sake of my relationships and overall well-being.

This realization marked the start of a major change in my life. The feelings of guilt and regret I experienced were intense, but they sparked a strong desire for change. I knew I had to confront and address the jealousy that had become so intertwined with who I was and how I acted. This internal acknowledgment was crucial in setting the stage for meaningful transformation.

From that point on, I began a journey of self-reflection and learning to manage my emotions effectively. I realized that my jealousy was connected to deeper, unresolved issues within me, such as insecurities and past experiences that I had not fully processed. I committed to understanding where these feelings originated and to separating my own emotions from those influenced by external sources. This introspective process was both challenging and enlightening, revealing layers of my emotional makeup that I had previously ignored.

This journey wasn't about pushing my feelings away or pretending they didn't exist. Instead, it was about embracing them, understanding their roots, and learning how to handle them in a healthy and constructive way. I focused on changing my thoughts and energy, breaking free from the destructive cycle of envy and bitterness that had long controlled my life. By shifting my mindset and cultivating a more positive outlook, I began to reclaim my emotional freedom.

As time went on, the grip of jealousy on my life started to loosen. Although I still felt moments of envy or insecurity, they no longer controlled my actions or dictated my emotions as they once did. I learned to recognize these feelings, understand what triggered them, and respond to them in a constructive manner. This newfound emotional resilience allowed me to navigate relationships with greater empathy and understanding, fostering healthier and more fulfilling connections.

This experience taught me invaluable lessons about the power of self-awareness. It showed me how essential it is to recognize when we are influenced by outside energies and beliefs, and the immense strength that comes from taking back control of our own emotional world. By becoming more mindful of my thoughts and emotions, I was able to create a more balanced and harmonious inner state, enhancing both my personal well-being and my interactions with others.

In my work with others, I've seen similar changes. By dealing with and letting go of negative energies and emotions, people often experience significant improvements in their well-being and outlook. It's about shedding the influence of external factors and reconnecting with their true selves, fostering a sense of inner peace and authenticity. This shared journey highlights the universal struggle with jealousy and the transformative power of overcoming it.

Jealousy, which once caused me pain and conflict, became a source of growth and enlightenment. It taught me that finding inner peace and happiness often involves facing our darkest emotions head-on. By confronting, understanding, and transforming these feelings, we open ourselves up to a deeper level of emotional freedom and spiritual connection. This journey of overcoming jealousy is a powerful example of self-reflection and emotional strength, illustrating the profound impact that addressing our negative emotions can have on our overall growth and fulfillment.

The journey of overcoming jealousy is a testament to the resilience of the human spirit. It's a call to explore our emotions deeply, understand their origins, and choose a path of healing and growth. By doing this, we free ourselves from the hold of negative emotions and unlock the potential for a more authentic, fulfilling, and joyful life. Embracing this emotional journey allows us to transform jealousy from a source of pain into a catalyst for profound personal and spiritual development, leading us toward a more harmonious and enriched existence.

Chapter 15:
The Influence of Thoughts and Beliefs on Our Reality

Our thoughts and beliefs have a powerful effect on the reality we experience. As we move through life, we are not just passive observers but active creators of our own experiences. The way we think and what we believe shape the world around us and influence how we live our lives. This profound connection underscores the importance of cultivating positive and empowering thoughts and beliefs to manifest a fulfilling and harmonious existence.

One of the most significant moments in my journey occurred during a deep meditation session. While sitting quietly, I felt a strong yet gentle pressure at my third eye—the space between my eyebrows. This sensation was more than just physical; it felt like a spiritual sign, reminding me of my connection to something much bigger than myself. It made me realize that I am part of a vast, interconnected universe. This profound experience brought a deep sense of self-love and belonging, lifting me out of feelings of isolation and loneliness, and fostering a newfound appreciation for my place in the cosmos.

This awakening highlighted the crucial role of self-love in our lives. Without it, we often perceive the world in a distorted way, feeling disconnected and alone. Embracing self-love helps us align with the positive, harmonious energies of the universe, creating a more fulfilling and connected experience. It serves as a foundation for building strong, healthy relationships with ourselves and others, enhancing our overall well-being and spiritual growth.

Another important lesson I learned was the value of surrender—letting go of control and trusting in the unseen forces that guide us. When we face situations where our understanding seems limited, practicing surrender allows us to follow higher wisdom and intuition. This approach transforms our experiences, aligning us with the natural flow of the universe. Surrender becomes not an act of giving up, but a conscious choice to align with a greater purpose, fostering inner peace and resilience.

These experiences highlight how our thoughts and beliefs shape our reality. Self-love and surrender are not just abstract ideas; they are practical tools that influence our lives in tangible ways. They act like magnets, drawing in situations and opportunities that match our inner state, thereby enhancing our ability to attract positive experiences and overcome challenges. By fostering a mindset of self-love and practicing surrender, we create a conducive environment for personal and spiritual growth.

Being aware of our thoughts and feelings gives us the power to handle life's challenges more effectively. When we observe our emotions during interactions with others, we see them as chances for growth and self-reflection. By stepping back and observing, we can avoid getting caught up in negative emotions and respond in a more positive and constructive way. This mindfulness allows us to maintain emotional balance and foster healthier, more meaningful relationships.

Humor has been incredibly helpful in managing tension and anger. Finding the funny side in difficult situations can disrupt negative energy and create space for calm and reflection. Laughter helps break the cycle of negativity and brings lightness to our interactions, promoting a more relaxed and harmonious atmosphere. Incorporating humor into our lives enhances our ability to cope with stress and fosters a sense of joy and resilience.

Recording conversations, especially during conflicts, has also been a valuable tool. Listening to these recordings helps us see our patterns and reactions more clearly. This awareness is the first step toward change, allowing us to understand our habits and their impact on our reality. By identifying and addressing negative patterns, we can cultivate more positive and effective ways of communicating and interacting with others.

Recognizing the impact of our thoughts and beliefs means stepping into our role as creators of our own reality. By cultivating self-love, practicing surrender, and being mindful of our thoughts, we create a reality filled with higher consciousness and positive energy. Our journey becomes an opportunity to paint our experiences with the colors of awareness, compassion, and connection, enriching our lives and those around us.

Every moment offers a chance to shape our reality. We have the power to choose the stories we tell ourselves, the beliefs we hold, and the vibrations we send out into the world. By doing so, we open ourselves up to a life that reflects our true nature's beauty, complexity, and depth. Embracing this power empowers us to live authentically and purposefully, creating a reality that aligns with our highest aspirations and deepest values.

In essence, understanding the influence of thoughts and beliefs on our reality empowers us to take control of our lives. It encourages us to cultivate a positive mindset, let go of limiting beliefs, and embrace practices that foster emotional and spiritual well-being. By doing so, we become conscious architects of our own destiny, shaping a reality that resonates with our true selves and contributes to a more harmonious and enlightened world.

Chapter 16:
Practical Steps for Reshaping Our Belief Systems

Changing our belief systems can be a powerful and life-changing journey. Our beliefs shape how we see the world, influence our feelings, and affect our actions. By updating these beliefs, we can transform our life experiences. Here are practical steps to guide you through this important process:

Awareness and Self-Reflection: The first step is to notice your current beliefs. Take some time to think about what you believe about yourself, others, and the world. Look for any beliefs that might be holding you back or making you feel negative. Recognize how these beliefs affect your life.

Questioning Beliefs: Examine your beliefs closely. Ask yourself why you hold these beliefs, where they came from, and if they are based on real facts or just assumptions. This step helps you start letting go of beliefs that no longer benefit you.

Seeking Alternative Perspectives: Open yourself to different viewpoints and cultures. By learning about other perspectives, you can challenge your existing beliefs and see the world in a new way. This is key to developing a more open and inclusive outlook.

Positive Affirmations: Replace limiting beliefs with positive affirmations. Create affirmations that match the new beliefs you want to adopt. Repeat these affirmations regularly to help them become a natural part of your thinking.

Visualization: Use visualization to strengthen your new beliefs. Picture yourself living in line with these beliefs and acting according to them. Visualization helps make these new beliefs feel more real and solid.

Surrounding Yourself with Positivity: The people and environment around you greatly affect your beliefs. Choose to be around positive influences and supportive people who encourage your growth and new beliefs.

Mindfulness and Meditation: Practice mindfulness and meditation to stay present and aware. These practices help you recognize and let go of negative thoughts that come from old beliefs.

Journaling: Keep a journal to record your thoughts, feelings, and progress. Writing things down helps with self-reflection and tracking how your beliefs are changing over time.

Seek Guidance: Don't hesitate to get help from mentors, coaches, or therapists. They can offer valuable insights and strategies for reshaping your beliefs effectively.

Celebrate Small Wins: Acknowledge and celebrate your progress, no matter how small it may seem. Celebrating these small victories boosts your motivation and reinforces the positive changes.

Patience and Persistence: Changing deep-seated beliefs takes time and effort. Be patient with yourself and stay committed to the process, even if progress feels slow.

Forgiveness and Release: Forgive yourself and others for past actions influenced by old beliefs. Letting go of these emotional burdens is crucial for moving forward and embracing new beliefs.

Affirming Your Worthiness: Believe in your inherent worthiness and that you deserve happiness, success, and fulfillment. Recognize your power to shape your reality and create a life that aligns with your true potential.

Consistency: Consistently applying these steps is essential for transforming your beliefs. Make these practices part of your daily routine to reinforce the changes.

Integration: Actively incorporate your new beliefs into your everyday life. Make choices and take actions that reflect these beliefs to make them a solid part of your reality.

Reshaping your belief system is not a quick or

straightforward process. It's a journey of ongoing growth and self-improvement. As you shed outdated and limiting beliefs and embrace empowering ones, you change how you see the world and open up new possibilities for living and interacting with others. By following these practical steps, you can navigate this transformative journey and create a belief system that aligns with your true potential and dreams.

Chapter 17:
Differentiating Between Physical and Spiritual Energies

In the world of energy healing and spiritual growth, it's essential to understand the distinction between physical and spiritual energies. These two types of energy are interconnected yet possess distinct qualities that influence how we experience life. Recognizing and appreciating their differences allows us to harness their unique benefits and maintain a balanced existence.

Physical energy is the kind of energy we can see and measure. It encompasses the energy within our bodies, the forces that drive the universe, and the electromagnetic interactions between physical objects. This energy is governed by scientific rules and the laws of physics, providing a tangible foundation for our daily lives. It powers our bodily functions, drives our technology, and keeps the planets and stars in motion. Physical energy is fundamental to our survival and the functioning of the material world, offering a concrete aspect to our existence.

Spiritual energy, on the other hand, is intangible and cannot be measured or seen through conventional means. It is deeply connected to our inner experiences, emotions, and intuition. This energy is personal and subjective, representing our connection to something greater than ourselves, such as the divine or the mystical realm. Spiritual energy is often associated with higher states of consciousness, fostering feelings of love, peace, and joy that elevate our spiritual awareness and inner growth.

One major difference between these types of energy is their vibration. Physical energy vibrates at frequencies that we can observe and measure, creating different physical effects that are tangible and studyable. Spiritual energy vibrates at much higher frequencies, which are usually beyond what we can perceive with our senses. These higher vibrations are linked to profound emotional and spiritual states, enhancing our ability to connect deeply with ourselves and the universe.

The sources of these energies also set them apart. Physical energy typically originates from external sources like the sun, food, and other environmental factors, adhering to the principles of energy conservation. In contrast, spiritual energy is believed to emanate from a universal or divine source. It is considered an infinite and ever-present force that permeates all aspects of existence, providing us with inspiration, creativity, and a sense of inner growth.

Even though physical and spiritual energies are different, they are inherently connected. They both play pivotal roles in our lives and significantly impact our overall well-being. The physical world offers the concrete aspects of our existence, while the spiritual world provides a space for inner exploration and growth. This synergy between the two allows us to lead a more holistic and enriched life, where our material needs are met alongside our spiritual aspirations.

To achieve true health and balance, we must honor and harmonize both physical and spiritual energies. Ignoring one type of energy can lead to imbalances and issues in our lives. For example, focusing solely on physical needs while neglecting our spiritual side can result in feelings of emptiness or lack of fulfillment. Conversely, concentrating exclusively on spiritual matters without addressing our physical needs can hinder our ability to function effectively in daily life.

From my experience with energy healing, I've learned the profound importance of balancing these energies. By integrating both physical and spiritual energies, we can live more harmoniously and reach our full potential in every area of life. This integration involves nurturing our bodies with proper care and also tending to our spiritual practices, such as meditation, mindfulness, and connecting with nature. Embracing both energies allows us to experience a deeper sense of well-being and fulfillment, fostering growth and resilience.

Embracing both physical and spiritual energies means paying close attention to the subtle changes in our experiences and understanding their significance. It involves recognizing that our physical experiences are intertwined with our spiritual journey, providing opportunities for growth and deeper self-understanding. By maintaining this awareness, we can navigate life's challenges with greater ease and cultivate a more profound connection with ourselves and the world around us.

As we explore our lives, knowing the difference between physical and spiritual energies helps us better understand ourselves and the world around us. It enhances our ability to feel connected to everything, guiding us on a path of self-discovery and spiritual growth. This comprehensive understanding empowers us to create a balanced and fulfilling life, where both our material and spiritual needs are met in harmony.

Chapter 18:
Tapping into Spiritual Frequencies for Guidance and Healing

Starting the journey to connect with spiritual frequencies for guidance and healing has been both eye-opening and deeply rewarding. This journey unfolds in different stages, each bringing new insights and connections with the unseen forces that shape our lives. A key moment in this journey occurred when I was in my early twenties. At that time, I began to realize what it meant to be an empath, someone who is highly sensitive to the emotions of others. This newfound awareness marked the beginning of a profound exploration into the depths of my emotional and spiritual landscape.

My understanding of being an empath transformed drastically after a conversation with someone who possessed psychic abilities. They helped me see that as a "super empath," I was constantly picking up on the emotions of the people around me. This heightened sensitivity often left me feeling overwhelmed and drained because it was challenging to distinguish between my own feelings and the emotions I was absorbing from others. It felt as though I was losing myself in a vast sea of external feelings, making it difficult to maintain my own emotional balance and sense of self.

This realization was a significant turning point for me, igniting a deep desire to explore the spiritual world more thoroughly to understand the different energies I was encountering. I needed to discern whether the thoughts and feelings I was experiencing were truly my own or if they were influenced by external spiritual energies. This quest for clarity was essential for my personal growth and emotional well-being.

To gain some clarity, I sought a clear sign from the spiritual realm—something unmistakable that would help me differentiate my thoughts from spiritual messages. The response I received was as surprising as it was enlightening. I woke up one morning with the vivid image of a small gecko in my mind. This Geico gecko, although not physically present, spoke to me with an Australian accent. It was a quirky and unexpected guide that began to offer me advice and insights, adding a touch of humor and lightness to my spiritual journey. This playful interaction made the process of connecting with spiritual frequencies more approachable and less intimidating, demonstrating that guidance can come in unexpected and delightful forms.

Having this guide around was a constant source of spiritual communication, though it came with its own set of challenges. Sometimes, the gecko's use of Australian slang left me confused, highlighting that spiritual messages can be influenced by cultural nuances and emphasizing the need for clarity in these communications. This experience taught me the importance of being open-minded and adaptable when interpreting spiritual signs, as well as the value of patience and persistence in understanding their true meanings.

From this experience, I learned the critical importance of discernment in spiritual communication. Even though the messages from my gecko guide were coming from a higher source, I had to interpret them carefully to ensure they fit into my understanding and reality. This discernment process was essential for integrating spiritual guidance into my daily life in a meaningful and effective way.

As my journey continued, I became increasingly interested in the concept of frequencies. I delved into both their scientific and spiritual aspects, discovering that everything—whether it's a physical object, a thought, or an emotion—vibrates at certain frequencies. This insight deepened my understanding of how everything in the universe is interconnected and how our thoughts and emotions influence our reality. By aligning myself with higher vibrational frequencies, I discovered that profound healing and transformation were possible. When our thoughts and intentions are tuned to these higher frequencies, they can greatly improve our well-being and spiritual growth, creating a harmonious balance between our inner and outer worlds.

Another important part of my journey was recognizing and following synchronicities—meaningful coincidences that seemed to guide me. These synchronicities included chance encounters with insightful people and events that occurred at just the right time. They served as gentle reminders from the universe, encouraging me to stay attentive and trust the process of my journey. Embracing these synchronicities reinforced my belief in the interconnectedness of all things and the presence of a guiding intelligence in our lives.

Exploring spiritual frequencies is an ongoing adventure of curiosity, discernment, and a deeper connection with unseen energies. It's a path filled with humor, mystery, and significant changes. Through this journey, I've come to realize that we are all deeply connected to the spiritual fabric of the universe. By tapping into these frequencies, we can gain a deeper understanding of ourselves and the world around us, fostering a sense of unity and purpose that enhances our overall well-being.

Tapping into spiritual frequencies for guidance and healing is more than just looking for external signs or validation. It's about developing an inner awareness of how we are influenced and guided by the energies around us. This journey encourages us to trust our intuition, believe in the unseen, and remain open to the possibilities of spiritual growth and transformation. As we walk this path, we learn to align with the rhythms of the universe, leading to a more fulfilled and spiritually enriched life. Embracing this connection allows us to navigate our spiritual journey with confidence, resilience, and a profound sense of purpose, ultimately guiding us toward a harmonious and enlightened existence.

Through the Eyes of an Energy Healer

CHAPTER 19:
UNRAVELING THE THREADS OF FEAR

Fear is something that has always been with us, as old as humanity itself. It's deeply embedded in our nature, originally helping our ancestors survive. In the earliest days, fear was a critical tool. It warned our ancestors about immediate threats like wild animals or dangerous weather, helping them stay alive. This primal fear was essential for survival, acting as an instinctual alarm system that kept early humans safe from harm.

But as humans developed and societies grew, the nature of fear changed. It became more complex and intertwined with our expanding understanding of the world. Fear was no longer just about physical dangers; it began to manifest in psychological and emotional forms. These new kinds of fear were not always related to immediate threats but were deeply rooted in our minds, reflecting our evolving consciousness and societal structures. Fear transformed from a basic survival mechanism into a multifaceted emotion that influences various aspects of our lives.

The way fear evolves is closely tied to how our minds develop. From the time we are young, our experiences shape how we see the world. Some fears stem from our early experiences or are inherited from those around us. These fears often hide in our subconscious, quietly guiding our reactions and decisions without us even realizing it. This subconscious influence means that fear can affect us in subtle yet profound ways, impacting our behavior and choices long after the initial fear-inducing event has passed.

As societies and cultures have changed, so has fear. Various institutions, like governments or the media, have played a significant role in shaping what we fear. These societal fears might not always come with a real, physical threat but can still have a big impact on our emotions and decisions. Media portrayals, for instance, can amplify fears about safety, health, and the future, creating a pervasive sense of anxiety that influences public perception and personal well-being.

Today, fear shows up in many different ways in our lives. It's not just about dangerous situations but also about social pressures, personal relationships, and the constant stream of information we receive from the digital world. Even though these modern fears might not always involve real physical danger, they still affect us deeply, holding us back and shaping how we see the world. The omnipresent nature of digital information means that fear can be triggered instantly and persistently, making it a significant factor in our daily emotional landscape.

Our ability to sense emotions, similar to animals and young children, shows how fear affects us and our surroundings. Children and animals can pick up on the fear and anxiety around them, demonstrating how connected we all are through our emotions. This sensitivity highlights the importance of emotional intelligence and the need to develop strategies to manage fear effectively, ensuring it does not overwhelm our capacity to thrive.

To deal with fear, it's important to understand where it comes from and how it has evolved. By distinguishing fears that are based on real dangers from those that are not, we can start to free ourselves from fear's control. This discernment is crucial for personal empowerment, allowing us to address and mitigate irrational fears while respecting and responding appropriately to genuine threats.

Facing fear involves making a conscious effort to question its validity. Practices like mindfulness and meditation are invaluable here. They help us observe our fears without being overwhelmed by them, giving us a clearer view and more control over our emotional responses. By cultivating a mindful presence, we can create a space where fear can be acknowledged and understood, rather than allowing it to dictate our actions and decisions.

Fear shouldn't be ignored or dismissed. Rational fears are helpful; they alert us to potential dangers and help us stay safe. But irrational fears, which often arise from misunderstandings or outside influences, need to be confronted and overcome. Addressing these fears involves self-reflection and a willingness to challenge and change limiting beliefs. This process helps us reach our full potential, as we are no longer held back by unfounded anxieties.

Breaking free from fear is a journey of self-discovery and empowerment. It means recognizing that we have the power to choose how we react to fear. Instead of letting fear define us, we learn to see it as just one part of our emotional experience. By building resilience, self-awareness, and a better understanding of our fears, we can change how we relate to this ancient emotion. This transformation allows us to embrace life more fully, moving forward with confidence and inner strength.

This journey can lead us to a place of bravery and true self-understanding. Fear no longer dictates our actions; instead, it can become a driver for personal growth and exploration. As we work through this, we embrace our inner strength and resilience, leading to a life filled with courage, compassion, and a deeper connection with who we really are. This enhanced relationship with fear enables us to navigate life's challenges with grace and wisdom, fostering a sense of peace and empowerment that enriches our overall existence.

In summary, unraveling the threads of fear involves a deep and ongoing process of self-awareness, understanding, and transformation. By confronting and addressing our fears, we unlock the potential for a more authentic and fulfilling life. This journey not only helps us overcome the barriers that fear creates but also empowers us to harness our emotions as tools for growth and self-improvement, ultimately leading to a more balanced and harmonious existence.

Through the Eyes of an Energy Healer

CHAPTER 20:
THE MULTIDIMENSIONAL SELF

When we explore who we are, we often focus on the physical world around us. We think about our bodies, our surroundings, and the everyday experiences we have. But there's a lot more to us than just what we can see and touch. There's a part of us that goes beyond the physical— this is called the multidimensional self. Understanding this concept opens up a new realm of self-awareness and spiritual growth, allowing us to connect with deeper aspects of our existence.

The idea of the multidimensional self suggests that we don't just exist in one single reality. While our physical bodies live in the material world, our consciousness, which is the essence of who we are, exists across different levels or planes of reality. This means that our awareness and being are connected to many different dimensions, not just the one we experience with our five senses. These dimensions may include emotional, mental, and spiritual planes, each contributing to our overall experience of life.

I first started to understand this idea when I began working with different frequencies in a special chamber. In this chamber, I explored how different vibrations affected both my body and mind. I could feel how some frequencies made me feel more alive and energized, while others didn't seem to have much effect. This hands-on experience was pivotal in illustrating the tangible impact that vibrational energy can have on our multidimensional selves.

For instance, I found that frequencies like 10 Hz and 20 Hz had a strong impact on me. The 10 Hz frequency, in particular, helped open up pathways in our cells that are important for creating energy. This was a big discovery because it showed me that certain frequencies could help heal and revitalize our bodies. It demonstrated how specific vibrational energies can interact with our physical form, promoting healing and enhancing our overall vitality.

As I continued to work with frequencies, I came across something called harmonics. Harmonics are like the layers of sound you hear in music. When you mix different frequencies, they create new patterns of sound that can resonate with different parts of us, helping to bring balance and healing. This layering of sounds mimics the complexity of our own energy fields, where multiple energies interact to create a harmonious whole. Understanding harmonics deepened my appreciation for the intricate ways in which sound and vibration can influence our well-being.

This is similar to what happens when you hit a gong. A gong produces a range of frequencies that interact with our energy field in different ways. This shows how sound and vibrations can help us heal and feel balanced, touching on various parts of our multidimensional selves. The rich, resonant tones of the gong facilitate a meditative state, allowing us to access deeper levels of consciousness and promote inner harmony.

One particular frequency I explored was 639 Hz, which is connected to the heart. By working with this frequency, I learned how focusing on specific areas of our being can create a harmonious vibration that affects our whole multidimensional nature. So, engaging with the right frequencies can help us connect with our entire being, not just one part. This targeted approach enhances our ability to heal specific aspects of ourselves, fostering a more integrated and balanced state of being.

Understanding our multidimensional self means recognizing that we are more than just our physical bodies. We are complex beings capable of connecting with and being influenced by many different energies and frequencies. This awareness opens up many possibilities for healing, personal growth, and a deeper connection with everything around us. It encourages us to explore beyond the surface, delving into the layers of our existence that contribute to our true essence.

As we learn more about these different realms, we can use this knowledge to improve our well-being. We can find and align with vibrations that support our health, clarity, and spiritual development. We also begin to connect with a larger collective consciousness, gaining insights and wisdom that go beyond our individual experiences. This collective awareness fosters a sense of unity and interconnectedness, enhancing our ability to contribute positively to the world around us.

Exploring our multidimensional self is not just about discovering more about ourselves but also about reconnecting with the universe. It helps us understand our place in the grand scheme of things and how we can harmonize with the energies that fill our existence. By embracing our multidimensional nature, we can gain a richer understanding of reality and our role within it. This journey leads to a more profound sense of purpose and a deeper connection with the cosmic forces that guide our lives.

In short, recognizing and engaging with our multidimensional self is a significant step towards living a more complete and connected life. It allows us to go beyond the limits of the physical world and fully experience all aspects of our being. As we explore this journey, we uncover new ways to heal, grow, and deepen our connection with the universe, enriching our lives in many meaningful ways. This holistic understanding empowers us to navigate life with greater insight and embrace the full spectrum of our existence.

Chapter 21:
Exploring Energy Healing Modalities

Energy healing is a captivating field with diverse approaches aimed at enhancing our well-being and spiritual growth. Each method operates on the principle that energy plays a crucial role in our health and overall balance. Through my journey, I have delved into various techniques, beginning with Reiki and expanding to other forms of energy healing. Despite their differing names and practices, these modalities all strive to balance and harness energy for healing purposes, each rooted in rich historical traditions that have evolved over centuries.

Reiki is perhaps the most well-known energy healing method. Originating from Japan in the early 20th century, Reiki was developed by Mikao Usui. Reiki focuses on channeling universal life energy to facilitate healing in the body and mind. The principle behind Reiki is that blockages in our energy can lead to imbalances and health issues. Practitioners use their hands to guide this energy, promoting relaxation, reducing stress, and fostering overall healing. Reiki quickly spread beyond Japan, gaining international recognition and becoming a cornerstone in many holistic healing practices today.

Acupuncture, a cornerstone of Traditional Chinese Medicine (TCM), is another ancient practice with a rich history dating back over 2,500 years. This technique involves inserting very fine needles into specific points on the body to balance the flow of Qi (or Chi), the vital life energy in TCM. By addressing disruptions in Qi, acupuncture seeks to restore balance and promote health. Historically, acupuncture was documented in the Huangdi Neijing (The Yellow Emperor's Classic of Medicine), which laid the foundational theories for meridians and energy pathways that are still used today. Acupuncture has since been integrated into various medical systems worldwide, recognized for its effectiveness in pain management and overall wellness.

Crystal healing is a method that employs the unique vibrations of crystals and gemstones. This practice has roots in ancient civilizations such as Egypt, where crystals were used for protection and healing, and in the Indigenous cultures of the Americas, where they were integral to spiritual rituals. Each crystal is believed to emit a specific frequency that interacts with our energy field. This interaction can help clear blockages, align chakras, and support spiritual growth. Modern crystal healing continues to draw on these ancient traditions, utilizing a wide array of stones to address different aspects of physical and emotional health.

Sound healing harnesses the power of sound and vibration for therapeutic purposes. Instruments such as singing bowls, gongs, and tuning forks produce specific sound frequencies that resonate with our energy field. This practice has historical significance in many cultures, including Tibetan Buddhism, where singing bowls are used in meditation practices, and in ancient Greece, where music was considered essential for health and harmony. These vibrations can lead to deep relaxation and realignment of our energy, promoting a state of balance and healing.

Energy psychology, which includes techniques like Emotional Freedom Techniques (EFT) and Thought Field Therapy (TFT), explores how our emotions and thoughts impact our energy. Developed in the late 20th century, EFT combines elements of cognitive therapy and exposure therapy with acupressure. These methods involve tapping on certain body points while focusing on emotional issues or limiting beliefs, aiming to release emotional blockages and improve emotional well-being. Energy psychology has gained popularity for its effectiveness in treating anxiety, PTSD, and other emotional disturbances.

Shamanic healing, rooted in indigenous traditions worldwide, connects with the spiritual realm and nature. Shamans perform rituals and ceremonies, often embarking on spiritual journeys to address physical, emotional, or spiritual problems. This approach emphasizes the interconnectedness of all living things and the importance of balance and harmony. Historically, shamans have been central figures in their communities, serving as healers, spiritual guides, and mediators between the human and spirit worlds.

Pranic healing, developed by Master Choa Kok Sui in the 20th century, works with prana, or life force energy. Building on ancient yogic and Buddhist principles, Pranic healing focuses on removing congested energy and infusing fresh, revitalizing energy into the body. The underlying principle is that maintaining balanced energy is crucial for health and healing. Pranic healing has been formalized into a structured system with specific protocols and techniques, making it accessible to a wider audience.

These examples represent just a few of the many energy healing practices available. Each modality brings its own methods and philosophies to working with energy, yet they all share the belief that energy is fundamental to our existence. Balancing and harmonizing this energy can lead to profound improvements in our health and well-being.

Exploring these different modalities provides a deeper understanding of how energy influences us and the world around us. Each practice offers a unique perspective and tools for healing, helping us to see ourselves not only as physical beings but also as energetic systems connected to the universe. This perspective empowers us to actively engage in our own healing and growth.

Integrating these practices into our daily lives can significantly enhance our well-being. Whether through regular Reiki sessions, incorporating crystals into our environment, or utilizing techniques from energy psychology, each method provides valuable tools for supporting our physical, emotional, and spiritual health. Embracing and exploring various energy healing modalities opens us to new possibilities for healing and deeper spiritual connection.

I have had the privilege of being mentored by notable figures such as James Van Praagh, Tamara Rose, Denise Linn, Gordon Smith, Abby Wynne, Dave Nelson, and Tania Rae. As a Certified Spiritual Healer, Certified Reiki Master, and Certified Elemental Space Clearer, I have also completed extensive training in Mediumship, Energy Healing, and Chakra Balancing and Clearing. These mentors have enriched my understanding and practice, allowing me to blend traditional techniques with modern insights.

While I am not a Psychic Medium, my work as a Psychic Energy Healer involves being guided by spirit energies and healing guides during sessions. My unique healing style, developed through guided meditations and direct contact with divine spirits, ensures that no two healing sessions are the same. Even though people who have passed often present themselves during sessions, I am more attuned to their present energies rather than their specific messages. This approach allows for a more fluid and personalized healing experience, tailored to each individual's unique energetic needs.

By exploring and embracing these diverse energy healing modalities, we can cultivate a holistic approach to health and spiritual growth, harnessing the power of energy to transform our lives in meaningful ways.

Through the Eyes of an Energy Healer

Chapter 22:
Finding Routines to Connect with Energy and Spirit

Finding a routine that deepens your connection with energy and Spirit can transform your daily life into a continuous dialogue with the divine. Each morning, I begin by expressing gratitude to Spirit for the new day. This simple act of acknowledgment sets a positive tone and opens the channel for spiritual connection, fostering a sense of appreciation and mindfulness from the very start of the day. My routine often includes a symbolic gesture of cleansing and preparation—standing under a shower, I let the water flow over me, visualizing it clearing and balancing each of my chakras. This visualization is not just a mental exercise; it serves as a powerful affirmation of my intention to maintain energetic harmony. This practice is particularly important when I have clients scheduled for the day. I ask Spirit to open and align my energy centers, ensuring that no personal or egoic interference affects my work, thereby creating a sacred space for healing and guidance.

Creating a list of things I'm grateful for is another cornerstone of my routine. Whether it's the simple pleasure of pancakes I enjoyed for breakfast or the privilege of working with several clients, recognizing these small blessings helps maintain a positive outlook. I remind myself that no matter how minor the gratitude, it contributes to a greater sense of connection and abundance. This daily gratitude practice not only enhances my mood but also attracts more positive experiences into my life, reinforcing a cycle of thankfulness and joy.

Before diving into my day, I take a moment to surrender control to Spirit. Instead of dictating every action and outcome, I simply say, "Here I am, Spirit. What do you have for me today?" This shift in perspective allows me to be guided rather than to control, trusting that Spirit will lead me through the day's events. This act of surrender cultivates a sense of trust and openness, enabling me to respond to life's challenges with grace and resilience.

Throughout the day, I periodically ask Spirit to raise my vibration, requesting healing for my mind, body, and soul. This practice ensures that my energy remains high and that I am protected from absorbing negative or lower vibrational energies from those around me. Being mindful of my energy field helps me maintain clarity and prevents me from being overwhelmed by the chaotic energies often encountered in everyday settings. By consistently realigning my energy, I create a protective barrier that supports my well-being and enhances my ability to provide effective healing to others.

One practical application of this awareness is during routine activities, such as shopping. When I walk through a store, I consciously stay in my own energy field, avoiding the chaos and energy of others around me. By maintaining this awareness, I can complete my tasks efficiently without feeling drained or scattered. This mindful approach transforms mundane activities into opportunities for maintaining energetic balance and reinforcing my connection with Spirit.

Incorporating meditation and mindfulness into my daily routine further supports my connection with Spirit. These practices help calm the mind and center my awareness in the present moment, creating a space where Spirit's guidance can emerge more clearly. Through meditation, I often receive insights and experience a profound sense of inner peace that enhances my spiritual connection. Mindfulness practices, such as focused breathing and body scanning, deepen my awareness of the present, allowing me to stay attuned to subtle spiritual signals throughout the day.

Spending time in nature is another powerful way to connect with Spirit. Whether it's a serene walk in the woods, a peaceful moment by the sea, or simply gazing at the stars, immersing myself in nature helps me feel a deep sense of unity with the universe. Nature serves as a tangible expression of Spirit, providing a direct and soothing connection to the divine. The natural rhythms and cycles I observe reinforce my understanding of the interconnectedness of all life, enhancing my spiritual awareness and fostering a sense of peace and belonging.

The journey to connect with Spirit also involves shedding layers of conditioning, fear, and limiting beliefs. This process of unpeeling veils of illusion allows for a clearer awareness of the divine presence within and around us. Confronting and understanding our fears as mere illusions opens the door to a deeper spiritual connection, freeing us from the constraints that hinder our growth. This transformative process requires courage and self-compassion, enabling us to embrace our true selves and align more closely with our spiritual essence.

An open heart is essential in this spiritual process. Embracing love, compassion, and gratitude aligns us with divine frequencies, allowing us to become conduits for spiritual energy. Approaching life with an open heart deepens our sense of oneness with all existence and enhances our connection with Spirit. Cultivating an open heart involves daily practices of kindness, forgiveness, and unconditional love, which help to dissolve barriers and foster a harmonious relationship with ourselves and others.

Engaging in spiritual practices and rituals—such as prayer, meditation, chanting, or sacred ceremonies—provides a structured way to connect with Spirit. These practices act as bridges between the physical and spiritual realms, offering glimpses into the unity that underlies all life. Rituals create sacred spaces where we can focus our intentions and energies, facilitating deeper spiritual connections and providing a sense of purpose and direction.

Reflecting on my personal journey, I recognize that connecting with Spirit is not a one-time event but an ongoing process of awakening and alignment. It is a path of continual discovery, surrender, and attunement to higher frequencies. This journey invites us to embrace the truth that we are part of a grand, interconnected cosmic tapestry, where every action and intention contributes to the greater whole.

In essence, connecting with Spirit is a journey of awakening. It is about recognizing our spiritual nature and understanding that our human journey offers opportunities for growth, healing, and the expansion of consciousness. By living with wonder, humility, and reverence, we seek answers not only in the external world but within the depths of our own being. This ongoing exploration reveals the profound truth that we have always been in the presence of the divine, inviting us to explore, grow, and embrace the fullness of our spiritual essence.

By establishing and maintaining these routines, we create a consistent and nurturing framework for our spiritual growth. These practices not only enhance our connection with Spirit but also cultivate a sense of inner peace, resilience, and purpose. As we integrate these routines into our daily lives, we embark on a transformative journey that enriches our existence and deepens our understanding of the spiritual dimensions that guide and support us.

Through the Eyes of an Energy Healer

CHAPTER 23:
A PROFOUND ENCOUNTER
WITH THE SOUL

During my journey of exploring energy healing and connecting with Spirit, there was one experience that stands out as truly life-changing. It was an encounter with the soul that shifted my understanding of healing in ways I never expected.

As a healer, I've always been fascinated by the concept of chakras. These are energy centers in our bodies that are believed to influence our physical, emotional, and spiritual well-being. Most traditional systems teach about seven main chakras, but I was guided to work with nine.

The two additional chakras I introduced into my practice were the Earth Star and the Soul Star. At the time, I didn't know much about these chakras; I had only heard a little about them. Yet, my intuition and guidance from Spirit encouraged me to include them in my healing work.

The Earth Star chakra is located below our feet, connecting us to the energy of the Earth. It helps us stay grounded and stable. On the other hand, the Soul Star chakra is positioned above our heads and is linked to our higher self and our connection to the divine.

When I started using these chakras in my healing sessions, something extraordinary began to happen. As I guided energy from the Earth Star up to the Soul Star, and used crystals and crystal bowls to enhance this energy, I began to witness an amazing phenomenon.

I started to see the soul of the person I was working with. It appeared like a cloud of light, somewhat like amber clouds drifting in front of the moon on a clear night. This cloud was the person's soul, and within it, I could see marks and scars.

These scars were not physical but were energetic imprints from past traumas, both from this life and previous ones. Each scar held a story—a wound that needed healing. It was as if the soul was showing me its history, its journey through time and space.

I could feel the emotions tied to these scars—pain, sorrow, fear, and sometimes even joy. It was a deeply emotional experience for me as a healer, because I knew that these scars represented the person's suffering. This profound understanding deepened my empathy and commitment to facilitate genuine healing.

As I continued the healing work, I saw some of

these scars slowly fade away, disappearing into the air. It seemed that simply acknowledging these scars and bringing them to light allowed them to be released and healed. The person receiving the healing often felt a significant sense of relief and lightness, as if a heavy burden was lifted from their spirit.

In some sessions, I noticed smaller clouds within the larger soul cloud. These smaller clouds had their own scars, representing the pain and suffering that the individual had absorbed from others in past lives. It was as if they had taken on others' burdens to help them heal. Clearing these smaller clouds was a crucial part of the healing process. It involved recognizing these imprints and gently letting them go, freeing the person from carrying burdens that were never theirs to bear. This aspect of healing emphasized the importance of releasing not only personal traumas but also inherited emotional baggage.

During these sessions, I also saw the presence of angels and other spiritual beings. They often appeared alongside the soul, bringing comfort, guidance, and a sense of divine love. These encounters with angelic beings reassured me that the healing process was being supported and guided by higher forces, providing a sense of security and assurance that I was not alone in this work.

One particularly memorable experience involved the appearance of winged horses. These magical creatures appeared during a session with a person who had a deep connection to horses. It felt as though the soul was expressing its love for these majestic animals, and the presence of the winged horses added a layer of beauty and meaning to the healing. This symbol of grace and freedom resonated deeply, enhancing the overall healing experience.

Reflecting on these experiences, I am reminded of how everything in life is interconnected. Our souls are not isolated; they are part of a vast, intricate web of existence. We carry the imprints of our own experiences and those of others who have touched our lives, illustrating the profound interconnectedness that defines our spiritual journey.

Connecting with the soul at this level is a sacred and deeply moving experience. It allows us to see the beauty, resilience, and wisdom of the human spirit. It shows us that healing involves more than just addressing physical or emotional symptoms; it's also about healing the wounds of the soul. This holistic approach to healing underscores the importance of nurturing all aspects of our being for true and lasting transformation.

In these moments of soul connection, I have witnessed tears, laughter, and a profound sense of liberation as people release the weight of their past. It's a reminder that healing is a multi-dimensional journey, touching on the physical, emotional, and spiritual aspects of our being. This comprehensive understanding of healing fosters a deeper sense of empathy and compassion, enhancing my ability to support others in their own healing processes.

This profound encounter with the soul has guided my healing path in unexpected ways. It has deepened my understanding of how everything is connected and the importance of addressing the root causes of suffering, not just the symptoms. By integrating this deeper awareness into my practice, I can offer more holistic and effective healing sessions that honor the full spectrum of the human experience.

As I continue to work with the Earth Star and Soul Star chakras, I am reminded of the incredible ability of the human spirit to heal, transform, and reconnect with the divine. This journey is one of self-discovery, self-love, and profound awakening—one that I am deeply grateful to be a part of. Embracing this path allows me to continually evolve as a healer, offering my clients not just physical or emotional relief, but also spiritual rejuvenation and a deeper sense of purpose.

Thus, this profound encounter with the soul has not only enhanced my understanding of healing but has also reinforced the importance of viewing each individual as a multi-dimensional being, deserving of comprehensive and compassionate care. It has affirmed that true healing lies in addressing all facets of the self, fostering a harmonious balance between the physical, emotional, and spiritual realms.

Through the Eyes of an Energy Healer

Chapter 24:
Implementing Energy Healing in Everyday Life

Energy healing isn't just something you do in a special place or during a dedicated session. It's something you can weave into your daily life to keep yourself balanced and aligned. Here are some practical ways to integrate energy healing into your everyday routines.

Every morning, as soon as I wake up, I start by expressing gratitude. I take a moment to thank Spirit for the new day and for the gift of life. This simple act of gratitude helps set a positive tone for the day and reminds me how everything is connected. Whether it's the pleasure of enjoying a good breakfast or the anticipation of working with clients, I find something to appreciate, no matter how small. This practice not only fosters a sense of thankfulness but also cultivates a mindset that attracts more positive experiences throughout the day.

During my morning routine, I practice clearing my energy. One of my favorite methods is to let water run over each of my chakras while I'm in the shower. I imagine the water washing away any negative or blocked energy from these centers. This visualization enhances the cleansing effect, helping me start the day with a clear and balanced energy field. If I have clients later, I also ask Spirit to help open their chakras, so they come to our sessions with an open heart and mind. This preparation ensures that both my energy and that of my clients are in harmony, facilitating effective healing.

Throughout the day, I keep a "grateful list." This list includes moments and experiences that bring me joy or make me smile. It might be something simple, like enjoying a delicious stack of pancakes, or something more significant, like having the chance to work with clients. The idea is to recognize and appreciate the beauty and abundance in everyday moments. Regularly updating this list reinforces a positive outlook and helps me stay focused on the good in my life, even amidst challenges.

A key part of my daily practice is surrendering to Spirit. Instead of planning every detail of my day, I trust that Spirit will guide me. I start my day by saying, "Here I am, Spirit. What do you have for me today?" This act of surrender helps me let go of the need to control everything and allows me to be open to divine guidance. I find that when I stop trying to control every aspect of my life, I'm better able to flow with life's natural rhythms and handle whatever comes my way with grace and resilience.

Protection is also important in my daily routine.

Before going out into the world, I visualize myself wrapped in a suit of protective light. This energy shield helps guard me from negative influences and keeps me grounded and centered throughout the day. However, no protection is perfect, so it's important to regularly cleanse and reset your energy to deal with any negativity that might still affect you. This ongoing maintenance ensures that I remain energetically balanced and capable of maintaining my well-being amidst external pressures.

Throughout the day, I also ask Spirit to raise my vibration. I believe that maintaining a high vibration is crucial for well-being. I request healing for my mind, body, and soul to cover all aspects of my being. This practice helps me stay aligned with higher frequencies of love, joy, and peace, which in turn attracts positive experiences and opportunities. By consciously elevating my vibration, I enhance my ability to respond to life's challenges with a positive and empowered mindset.

As an energy healer or empath, it's common to pick up on the energies of others. To manage this, I use a practice of energetically wiping myself down to release any residual energy from people I've interacted with during the day. This helps me keep my own energy clear and prevents me from carrying the emotional or energetic baggage of others. Regularly performing this cleansing ritual maintains my energetic integrity and ensures that I can continue to offer effective and compassionate healing to those I work with.

Another challenge many people face is dealing with the chaotic energy of crowded places like shopping centers. To handle this, I make a point to stay grounded and centered. When I enter a busy store, I set the intention to remain calm and move at my own pace. By doing this, I avoid getting caught up in the surrounding chaos and maintain a sense of inner peace. This mindful approach allows me to navigate crowded environments without feeling overwhelmed, preserving my energy and focus.

Incorporating energy healing into your daily life doesn't require complicated rituals. It's about being aware, practicing gratitude, setting intentions, and taking simple steps to protect and cleanse your energy. By doing this, you create a more harmonious and balanced life that reflects your true self and connects you to the higher energies of the universe. These daily practices not only support your physical and emotional health but also deepen your spiritual connection, fostering a sense of purpose and fulfillment that permeates every aspect of your existence.

By integrating these practices into your routine, you cultivate a supportive environment for continuous healing and spiritual growth. Whether through mindful mornings, ongoing gratitude, or intentional protection, each step contributes to a balanced and enriched life. Embracing these energy healing routines empowers you to maintain alignment with your highest self, enhancing your overall well-being and fostering a deeper connection with the universal energies that guide and sustain us.

CHAPTER 25:
THE ROLE OF ENERGY HEALERS
IN MODERN SOCIETY

Energy healers have an important role to play in today's world. I've found that being an energy healer is not just fulfilling but also essential, especially in our fast-paced and often stressful lives. Let's explore how energy healers contribute to our modern society and why their work is so valuable right now.

In our busy world, many people are looking for ways to find peace, balance, and healing. The constant demands of work, the overwhelming amount of information from technology, and the general rush of daily life can leave people feeling stressed, disconnected, and spiritually drained. This is where energy healers come in. We help people find a sense of calm and guide them on their journey to healing and self-discovery. By providing a sanctuary of tranquility amidst the chaos, energy healers offer a vital refuge where individuals can reconnect with their inner selves and restore their emotional equilibrium.

Energy healers work on multiple levels to help people heal. This includes physical, emotional, mental, and spiritual aspects. We understand that true healing goes beyond just fixing physical symptoms; it involves finding and addressing the deeper causes of imbalances and discomfort. Techniques like Reiki, acupuncture, chakra balancing, and sound therapy are used to restore balance to the body's energy systems, helping people feel better and stay healthy. These methods not only alleviate immediate ailments but also promote long-term wellness by ensuring that energy flows freely and harmoniously throughout the body.

Conventional medicine often focuses on treating symptoms rather than the root causes of issues. Energy healing provides a different approach by working with the body's subtle energy systems. This method supports the body's natural ability to heal itself. It recognizes that our physical health is deeply connected to our energetic well-being. By addressing energy blockages and imbalances, energy healers facilitate the body's intrinsic healing processes, complementing traditional medical treatments and enhancing overall health outcomes.

Another important role of energy healers is helping people release emotional and mental blockages. Many problems we face come from unresolved emotions, past traumas, and limiting beliefs. Through practices like energy clearing, emotional release, and guided meditation, healers help people let go of what holds them back. This process can lead to emotional healing and personal growth. By clearing these blockages, individuals can achieve greater mental clarity, emotional stability, and a more positive outlook on life, enabling them to pursue their goals with renewed vigor and confidence.

Energy healers also channel universal healing energy, sometimes called chi, prana, or ki. This energy is the life force that sustains all living things. By directing this healing energy, we can boost the body's natural healing abilities and support overall wellness. This universal energy acts as a bridge between the physical and spiritual realms, facilitating a deeper connection with the divine and enhancing the effectiveness of the healing process.

As energy healers, we act as a bridge between the physical world and the spiritual realm. We understand that our human experience is not just about the material world but is also connected to spiritual dimensions. By helping people connect with higher states of consciousness and divine guidance, we assist them in tapping into their own spiritual essence and inner wisdom. This connection fosters a sense of purpose and alignment, guiding individuals towards a more meaningful and fulfilling life.

Our work as energy healers also benefits communities and society at large. When we help individuals heal and transform, the positive effects ripple outwards. People who experience healing and personal growth are more likely to spread positive energy and compassion to others. This creates a supportive and nurturing community environment where collective well-being is prioritized and fostered.

Moreover, energy healers support the spiritual awakening and growth of humanity. We live in a time of significant shifts in consciousness, with more people seeking deeper meaning and purpose in their lives. As individuals awaken to their true selves and higher potentials, they become agents of positive change, contributing to the collective growth of humanity. This spiritual awakening leads to a more compassionate, empathetic, and harmonious society, where individuals are empowered to live authentically and contribute positively to the world.

In a society where material success and external achievements often overshadow inner growth, energy healers remind people of the importance of self-discovery and self-care. We encourage individuals to focus on their own well-being, connect with their inner wisdom, and maintain inner peace and balance. This emphasis on inner growth fosters a more resilient and emotionally intelligent population, capable of navigating life's challenges with grace and strength.

It's important to understand that energy healing is not meant to replace conventional medicine or other therapies but to complement and enhance them. Energy healing is a holistic approach that works alongside other treatments to support overall health and wellness. By integrating energy healing with traditional medical practices, individuals can achieve a more comprehensive and balanced approach to their health, addressing both physical and energetic aspects of well-being.

As energy healers, we are committed to our own personal growth and development. To be effective in our roles, we need to continually work on our own healing and spiritual growth. This dedication not only benefits us but also improves our ability to help others. By maintaining our own energetic balance and spiritual alignment, we ensure that we can provide the highest level of healing and support to those we serve.

Energy healers play a crucial role in modern society by offering a holistic approach to health and well-being. We address physical, emotional, mental, and spiritual needs, guiding individuals towards balance and self-discovery. Our work helps create harmony and contributes to the greater good of our communities and the world. In times when many are searching for meaning and connection, energy healers offer a valuable path to transformation and healing. By fostering a deeper understanding of energy and its impact on our lives, we empower individuals to take control of their own healing journeys and achieve a state of holistic well-being.

Chapter 26:
Sound in Universal Healing

Exploring the world of energy and frequency healing has led me to a fascinating discovery: sound has incredible power to heal and balance our entire being. My journey into the realm of vibrations has shown me just how important sound is for restoring and revitalizing our physical, emotional, and spiritual health. This profound understanding has deepened my appreciation for the subtle yet powerful ways in which sound interacts with our bodies and souls.

At its core, sound is simply vibration. It moves through the air, creating waves that can touch us deeply. Every sound we hear, whether it's the gentle rustling of leaves, the rhythmic beats of a drum, or the complex melodies of a symphony, is a vibration that interacts with our bodies. These vibrations can influence the many different frequencies within us, resonating with our energy centers and promoting harmony and balance. This intricate interplay between sound and our internal energy systems underscores the vital role that sound plays in our overall well-being.

This realization made me wonder: Can we use sound frequencies in a specific way to change and improve our body's energy patterns? This profound question inspired me to create something special—a dedicated space for exploring how sound can heal. I envisioned a place called the Frequency Healing Chamber, where sound waves would be meticulously designed to help people heal and find balance. This chamber would serve as a sanctuary for those seeking to harness the transformative power of sound in a controlled and intentional environment.

Imagine a room where the walls are equipped with advanced technology to produce precise sound frequencies. When you enter this chamber, you are surrounded by a cocoon of sound waves tailored to your specific healing needs. These carefully selected frequencies are intended to help align and heal your body, mind, and spirit, bringing them back to their natural state of harmony. The immersive sound environment creates a deeply therapeutic experience, allowing you to fully engage with the healing vibrations.

The Frequency Healing Chamber is the culmination of many years of research into how our bodies function and how different frequencies can affect us. Created with guidance from spiritual insights and visions, this chamber offers a unique experience that can't be found anywhere else. It embodies the perfect blend of scientific precision and spiritual wisdom, ensuring that each session is both effective and spiritually enriching.

The concept of the frequency chamber combines simplicity with depth. Just as musical instruments are meticulously tuned to produce the best sound, our bodies can be tuned to resonate with frequencies that promote well-being and balance. This space demonstrates the powerful role sound can play in realigning and healing us, providing a tangible method for achieving energetic harmony. By tuning into these specific frequencies, we can facilitate profound shifts in our energy states, enhancing our capacity for healing and personal transformation.

Inside the chamber, you would experience a rich and complex sound environment. The frequencies interact with your body's energy field, creating a harmonious dance at the cellular level and reaching into your conscious and subconscious mind. Each sound frequency acts like a key, unlocking and awakening your inner potential, and guiding you on a path of healing and discovery. This dynamic interaction fosters a deep sense of relaxation and openness, making it easier to release blockages and embrace healing energies.

Everyone's experience in the chamber will be different. For some, the sounds may help release old, stuck energy, facilitating the flow of fresh, vibrant energy throughout the body. For others, it might realign emotional patterns or reconnect them with their natural state of harmony. This personalized response ensures that each individual receives the specific healing they need, tailored to their unique energetic landscape. This process is both a return to and a discovery of the balance that is always within us, highlighting the innate capacity for self-healing and renewal.

This chamber isn't just a place for healing; it also connects ancient traditions with modern technology. It draws on old practices where sound was used in healing and spiritual rituals, such as the use of chanting, drumming, and singing bowls in various cultural ceremonies. By combining these timeless techniques with the latest advancements in sound technology, the Frequency Healing Chamber offers a powerful environment for holistic healing. This blend of ancient wisdom and modern science creates a synergistic effect, amplifying the healing potential of sound and making it accessible to a wider audience.

In essence, the Frequency Healing Chamber represents the broader potential of sound as a healing tool. Whether we are listening mindfully, chanting sacred sounds, or simply enjoying the natural symphony around us, we can use sound to heal, balance, and awaken spiritually. Sound is a universal language that transcends boundaries and speaks directly to our core. It is a language of vibrations and frequencies that holds the key to integrating and harmonizing our body, mind, and spirit. By embracing this universal language, we can unlock new pathways to healing and transformation, fostering a deeper connection with ourselves and the universe.

Sound's ability to penetrate deeply into our being makes it an invaluable tool for energy healing. By consciously using sound, we can influence our energy patterns, release stored tensions, and promote a state of holistic well-being. This chapter underscores the profound impact that sound can have on our healing journey, highlighting its role as a powerful catalyst for personal and spiritual growth.

Through the Eyes of an Energy Healer

Chapter 27:
Trusting Spirit and the Creation of the Frequency Healing Chamber

Trust is the foundation of all spiritual work. Without it, we are adrift, questioning every whisper, every nudge, and every sign that comes our way. For years, I had learned to place my faith in the guidance that Spirit provides. Yet, when the idea for the Frequency Healing Chamber first began to unfold, even I had moments of doubt. This uncertainty was natural, as embarking on such a transformative project required a deep level of faith and surrender.

The concept wasn't something I had consciously thought about; it came through in bits and pieces, seemingly random, but all connected by an underlying energy I didn't fully understand. Spirit whispered to me about sound, vibration, and harmonics, and I knew I was being asked to create something beyond my imagination. The complexity of what lay ahead was far greater than anything I had attempted before. But I trusted, and Spirit delivered. This trust was essential, as it allowed me to move forward despite the uncertainties, embracing the unknown with an open heart and mind.

The first program for the chamber took 800 hours to compose. At the start, I had no idea of the intricate harmonics that would emerge. As each modality worked individually and then harmonized together, new dimensions of healing frequencies unfolded—ones that could not have been consciously engineered by any human hand. Spirit had shown me the foundation, but it was as if I was watching it build itself with each layer of sound. The healing frequencies became a symphony of energy, where each note, each vibration, had a specific purpose. It was alive, pulsating with intention and guided by a wisdom beyond my own.

But the chamber is so much more than just sound. It integrates a variety of healing modalities that work in harmony, often creating their own spontaneous harmonics that resonate with the individual. It's as if the chamber itself becomes attuned to the unique energy of the person inside, responding and shifting in real time to meet their needs. Each modality—whether it be sound, light, energy work, or even breath—blends together to form an intricate web of healing frequencies. It's not just a tool; it's a living, breathing organism of healing potential, capable of adapting to the diverse needs of each person who enters.

What's remarkable is that these modalities don't just coexist—they interact. The way they intertwine creates a new layer of harmonics that often surpasses what each modality could achieve on its own. These harmonics are not random; they are deeply intelligent, aligning with the energy field of the individual to bring about healing on all levels—physical, emotional, mental, and spiritual. It's as if the chamber has its own definition of artificial intelligence, but not in the way we typically think of AI. Instead of being a product of human programming, it is Spirit-guided intelligence, an organic form of AI that knows exactly what each person needs at any given moment. This intelligent synergy enhances the effectiveness of the healing process, ensuring that each session is uniquely tailored to facilitate profound transformation.

During the creation process, I was guided by Spirit and received profound insight from one of the greatest minds of all time—Nikola Tesla. His spirit would appear during deep meditative states, offering guidance on the technical aspects of energy, frequency, and resonance. Tesla was a master of understanding the subtle yet powerful forces that govern the universe, and he imparted wisdom about the flow of energy in ways I had never considered. It was not just about the frequencies themselves but how they interacted with the human energy field, restoring balance and unlocking potential. Tesla's insights were invaluable, bridging the gap between ancient spiritual practices and modern scientific understanding, and enabling the creation of a chamber that operates on both intuitive and technical levels.

With Tesla's guidance, I realized that this chamber wasn't just a tool for healing—it was a doorway to higher consciousness. The frequencies tapped into realms of existence where time, space, and physical form no longer held the same meaning. Healing could happen not just in the body but across timelines, dimensions, and lifetimes. This expanded perspective allowed me to design the chamber in a way that facilitated multi-dimensional healing, addressing not only present ailments but also past and future imprints that influenced an individual's well-being.

Each frequency within the chamber carries a specific energetic blueprint, and when combined, they form harmonics that shift reality itself. The chamber became a space where one could enter and emerge transformed— an alchemical process of soul healing. This profound encounter with the soul has guided my healing path in unexpected ways. It has deepened my understanding of how everything is connected and the importance of addressing the root causes of suffering, not just the symptoms. As I continue to refine and expand the Frequency Healing Chamber, I remain committed to trusting Spirit's guidance, knowing that this creation is a powerful testament to the divine potential within each of us.

As Spirit continues to guide me, the Frequency Healing Chamber stands as a beacon of hope and transformation. It embodies the seamless integration of ancient wisdom and modern technology, offering a sanctuary where individuals can experience deep healing and spiritual awakening. This journey of creation has not only enhanced my own spiritual practice but has also provided a valuable resource for others seeking balance, healing, and a deeper connection with the universal energies that sustain us all.

Through the Eyes of an Energy Healer

Chapter 28:
The Frequency Chamber

The Frequency Healing Chamber is a special place designed to explore how sound and vibrations can heal and balance our bodies. This idea emerged from combining ancient wisdom with modern technology, inspired by the work of Nikola Tesla and other spiritual insights. Let's dive into what makes this chamber unique and how it can help us achieve profound healing.

To understand the Frequency Healing Chamber, it's important to know how sound and vibrations affect us. Sound is essentially a vibration that travels through the air and can touch us deeply. It's not just about the music we hear; every sound around us, from the wind rustling through leaves to the chirping of birds, is a vibration that affects our body and mind. These vibrations interact with our energy centers, influencing our physical, emotional, and spiritual states in subtle yet powerful ways.

I began to wonder if we could use these sound

vibrations intentionally to heal our bodies. This curiosity led to the idea of creating a space where sound frequencies could be used to improve our health and well-being. This space is what we now call the Frequency Healing Chamber. The chamber is meticulously designed to harness the healing potential of sound, creating an environment where individuals can experience deep relaxation and energetic realignment.

The Frequency Healing Chamber is much more than a room filled with sound; it is a space where multiple healing modalities work in harmony to create viable harmonics that cater to each individual's specific needs. These modalities, both ancient and modern, come together to create a profound healing experience. Let's explore the key modalities integrated into the chamber:

Multiwave Oscillator: This device generates multiple frequencies at once, helping to restore the body's natural electrical charge and promote overall healing.

Vibroacoustic Sound Therapy: Using low-frequency sound vibrations, this therapy stimulates deep tissue healing, relieves pain, and reduces stress.

Light Therapy: Specific wavelengths of light are used to target and heal different layers of the body, promoting balance and well-being.

Crystal Therapy: Crystals are used to amplify and direct healing energy, clearing blockages and aligning the body's energy centers.

UVB Narrowband Light: This specialized light therapy is effective for treating skin conditions and boosting the immune system.

Sound Therapy: The chamber's carefully tuned sound waves work with the body's energy field to balance, heal, and restore vibrational harmony.

Aromatherapy: Natural essential oils are diffused into the air, promoting relaxation, emotional balance, and overall well-being.

Color Therapy: Colors are used to affect the mind and body, each hue resonating with different emotional and physical states to restore balance.

Sacred Geometry: The ancient wisdom of geometric patterns is used to harmonize energy and create a balanced, healing space within the chamber.

Tensor Rings: These copper rings generate a subtle energy field that helps with healing, clearing, and balancing the body's energy.

Orgone Energy: Based on Wilhelm Reich's work, orgone energy devices are used to clear stagnant energy and support life force energy flow.

Reiki Healing: A hands-on healing technique that channels universal life force energy to promote balance and healing on all levels.

Each of these modalities is vital, but it is their combined interaction that makes the chamber so powerful. Together, they create unique harmonics that resonate with the individual's specific needs, allowing for profound healing and transformation. The chamber itself is a blend of ancient wisdom and modern technology, embodying an intelligence that seems almost sentient—a living, breathing system of energy that knows exactly what each person requires at that moment.

Imagine a room designed to use sound in a very specific way. The walls of this room are equipped with special devices called transducers, which can create precise sound frequencies. When you enter the chamber, you are surrounded by these carefully tuned sound waves. The idea is that these frequencies can help balance and heal your body, mind, and spirit, bringing them back to their natural state of harmony. The immersive experience provided by the chamber allows for a deep connection with the healing vibrations, facilitating a transformative journey toward wellness.

The Frequency Healing Chamber is built on a simple but profound concept: just like musical instruments need to be tuned to produce the best sound, our bodies can also be tuned to resonate with healing frequencies. When we are in this chamber, we experience a range of sounds that interact with our body's energy field. This interaction can help clear out old energy patterns, balance emotions, and reconnect us with our natural state of harmony. By tuning into these specific frequencies, we can facilitate profound shifts in our energy states, enhancing our capacity for healing and personal transformation.

Every person's experience in the chamber will be different. Some might feel a deep sense of relaxation, while others might experience emotional release or new insights about themselves. The goal is to use sound to unlock the body's potential for healing and self-discovery.

This personalized approach ensures that each individual receives the specific healing they need, tailored to their unique energetic landscape.

This chamber is also a bridge between old and new. It combines ancient practices where sound was used for healing and spiritual rituals with modern technology. In the past, people used sound in rituals and healing practices, and now we use advanced technology to harness these sounds more precisely. This blend of traditional wisdom and cutting-edge science creates a powerful environment for holistic healing, making the Frequency Healing Chamber a truly unique and effective space for anyone seeking to enhance their well-being through the power of sound.

Overall, the Frequency Healing Chamber shows us the amazing potential of sound as a tool for healing. Whether we are listening mindfully, chanting, or simply enjoying the natural sounds around us, engaging with sound intentionally can help us heal, find balance, and awaken spiritually. The chamber stands as a testament to the harmonious integration of ancient healing traditions and modern technological advancements, offering a sanctuary where individuals can experience the full spectrum of sound's healing capabilities.

CHAPTER 29:
THE MULTIWAVE OSCILLATOR

In the realm of energy healing, the Multiwave Oscillator (MWO) stands out as a remarkable tool designed to restore balance and vitality at the cellular level. This device harnesses the power of a wide array of frequencies, each tailored to impact the cells in unique and beneficial ways. Unlike other tools such as the Rife machine, which focuses primarily on targeting and eliminating pathogens, the MWO is engineered to invigorate and energize the body's cells, fostering a robust immune response and overall health.

At its core, the MWO operates on the principle of cellular resonance. Our bodies comprise over three trillion cells, each vibrating at its own distinct frequency. This concept of cellular resonance posits that when external frequencies are introduced, they can interact with and influence the natural vibrations of our cells. By emitting a range of frequencies, the MWO essentially tunes these cells, much like recharging a battery to restore its full potential. This holistic approach ensures that every cell receives the precise vibrational energy it needs to function optimally.

Consider each cell in your body as a miniature power station. These stations are responsible for maintaining health and balance, but just as any energy source can become depleted, so too can cells become drained due to factors such as stress, environmental toxins, and illness. This depletion can lead to compromised cellular function and overall health challenges. The MWO addresses this by delivering a spectrum of frequencies that target and rejuvenate these power stations, ensuring they operate at their highest efficiency.

Herein lies the significance of the MWO. By delivering a spectrum of frequencies, the device provides cells with the energy they need to rejuvenate. Picture it as a symphony of frequencies where each note plays a distinct role, targeting various aspects of the body to stimulate healing and restoration. This harmonious interaction helps cells regain their strength, improve their functionality, and restore balance. The result is a comprehensive enhancement of the body's natural healing processes, promoting long-term wellness and vitality.

The advantages of the MWO extend beyond mere physical revitalization. One of its most profound benefits is its ability to enhance the immune system. A well-functioning immune system is critical for defending against infections, viruses, and other harmful agents. When cells absorb the frequencies emitted by the MWO, they become more resilient and effective at warding off threats. This increased cellular vitality supports a stronger immune response, helping to keep the body healthy and better equipped to handle challenges. Additionally, the MWO aids in reducing inflammation and accelerating recovery, making it a valuable tool for those dealing with chronic conditions or injuries.

Another notable feature of the MWO is its ability to combine simplicity with effectiveness. Traditional medical treatments often target specific symptoms or conditions, but the MWO takes a more holistic approach. Instead of merely addressing isolated issues, it focuses on correcting underlying imbalances within the body. This comprehensive method allows for a more profound and lasting impact on overall health. By harmonizing the body's energy systems, the MWO not only alleviates current ailments but also prevents future imbalances, promoting sustained well-being.

The Multiwave Oscillator represents a significant advancement in energy healing. Its ability to recharge the body's cells, enhance immune function, and address systemic imbalances underscores its value as a holistic tool for restoring health and vitality. As our understanding of energy healing continues to evolve, the MWO remains a compelling example of how the principles of frequency and vibration can be applied to promote overall well-being and harmony within the human body. By integrating this technology into our healing practices, we embrace a powerful means of fostering balance and vitality, harnessing the full potential of energy to support and enhance our health.

The MWO not only revitalizes cells but also harmonizes the body's entire energy field, creating a state of equilibrium that is essential for optimal health. This intricate balance between different frequencies ensures that the body can efficiently perform its natural functions, leading to improved physical health, emotional stability, and spiritual clarity. As we continue to explore and utilize the capabilities of the Multiwave Oscillator, we unlock new dimensions of healing that empower us to live healthier, more balanced lives.

CHAPTER 30:
LIGHT THERAPY AND
CRYSTAL HEALING

In the world of holistic healing, two methods stand out for their ability to promote wellness and balance: Light Therapy and Crystal Healing. When used together, these methods create a powerful effect that enhances their individual benefits and provides a deeper healing experience.

Light Therapy uses specific wavelengths of light to help with various health issues. It's also called phototherapy. In the Frequency Chamber, this therapy is taken to the next level. Lights above the person shine with targeted wavelengths, surrounding them in healing light. This gentle yet effective illumination can help with many conditions, such as insomnia, attention deficit disorder (ADHD), dementia, and even motor functions in people with Parkinson's Disease. The precision of these light wavelengths ensures that each therapeutic session is tailored to address specific health concerns, maximizing the potential for healing and rejuvenation.

The Frequency Chamber is designed with lights placed strategically to maximize their therapeutic effects. When combined with Lemurian quartz crystals, the benefits of Light Therapy are further enhanced. Lemurian quartz crystals are known for their high vibrational energy and are believed to carry ancient wisdom and healing properties. These crystals work together with the light therapy, boosting its effects and helping people feel more relaxed and balanced. The synergy between the light and the crystals creates a harmonious environment that facilitates deeper healing and a greater sense of inner peace.

On its own, Crystal Healing is a practice that uses the natural properties of crystals to restore balance and promote overall well-being. In the Frequency Chamber, the crystal light therapy unit is central to this healing method. This unit sends out healing frequencies that align with the body's energy centers, known as chakras. This alignment helps to balance and harmonize the body's energy. Each crystal is carefully selected for its unique properties, ensuring that the energy it emits resonates perfectly with the intended healing frequency.

Combining Light Therapy and Crystal Healing in the Frequency Chamber creates a complete healing environment that addresses physical, emotional, and spiritual well-being. As a person relaxes on the massage table, they are bathed in the soothing glow of therapeutic light and surrounded by the subtle energy of Lemurian quartz crystals. This creates a deep sense of relaxation and rejuvenation, allowing the individual to fully immerse themselves in the healing process. The integrated approach ensures that all aspects of the person's being are nurtured and revitalized.

Additionally, the frequencies emitted by the crystal light therapy unit work together with those from the Multiwave Oscillator and other healing methods in the chamber. This blend of energies enhances the healing process, allowing for better balance and rejuvenation at the cellular level. The interconnectedness of these modalities ensures that the healing is comprehensive, addressing multiple layers of well-being simultaneously.

In summary, Light Therapy and Crystal Healing are powerful methods for promoting wellness and balance. When combined in the Frequency Chamber, they create a holistic approach to healing. By using the healing properties of light and the natural energy of crystals, this integrated method offers a comprehensive path to health and vitality. This synergy not only amplifies the individual benefits of each modality but also creates a unified healing experience that fosters profound and lasting transformation.

CHAPTER 31:
TENSOR RINGS

In the world of energy healing, Tensor Rings stand out as powerful tools for achieving balance, peace, and healing. These unique devices, inspired by the sacred geometry of the Great Pyramid of Giza, have the potential to change energy patterns, support spiritual growth, and enhance overall well-being. Their intricate designs and profound energetic properties make Tensor Rings indispensable in holistic healing practices.

Tensor Rings are simple yet significant structures made from copper wire shaped into specific geometric patterns. These shapes are based on the precise measurements used in the Great Pyramid, creating a special connection with the fundamental forces of the universe. This connection allows Tensor Rings to tap into a continuous flow of healing energy that is present in all living things, fostering an environment conducive to deep healing and transformation.

What makes Tensor Rings truly special is their ability to capture and strengthen subtle energies. They act as conduits for healing on physical, emotional, and spiritual levels. Unlike electrical or magnetic fields, the energy from Tensor Rings is unique and offers a gentle but effective influence on the surrounding energy environment. This subtle interaction ensures that the healing process is harmonious and non-intrusive, allowing for a natural restoration of balance.

One of the key features of Tensor Rings is their role as superconductors. They can neutralize electromagnetic fields and harmonize energy patterns that are out of balance. This quality makes Tensor Rings invaluable for creating sacred spaces, such as homes, healing centers, or meditation rooms, where people can experience deep relaxation, mental clarity, and spiritual renewal. By mitigating the effects of negative or chaotic energies, Tensor Rings help maintain a serene and supportive atmosphere.

In the Frequency Chamber, Tensor Rings play an essential role in enhancing the healing experience. By incorporating these rings into the chamber's design, we create an environment that feels almost like a portal to other dimensions, amplifying the transformative energies present in the space. The subtle yet powerful energy from the Tensor Rings works in synergy with other healing methods in the chamber, helping individuals feel more relaxed, balanced, and healed. This integration ensures that every aspect of the healing process is supported and amplified, providing a comprehensive and immersive healing experience.

From my personal experience, I can attest to the positive effects of Tensor Rings. In my home, I use a pyramid tensor set during my meditation practice to create a special space for deep reflection and healing. The gentle energies emitted by these rings help make the environment harmonious and supportive of meditation and self-discovery. This personal practice not only enhances my own well-being but also enriches the healing sessions I conduct with others.

Integrating Tensor Rings into the Frequency Chamber adds another layer of depth to the healing process. As people relax in the chamber, surrounded by soothing light, Lemurian quartz crystals, and the frequencies from the Multiwave Oscillator, the presence of Tensor Rings further boosts the healing potential of the space. This combination of modalities creates a powerful, multi-dimensional healing environment that addresses the needs of the body, mind, and spirit simultaneously.

In essence, Tensor Rings are powerful tools for healing and transformation, both inside the Frequency Chamber and in other settings. By connecting ancient wisdom from the Great Pyramid of Giza with modern healing techniques, these rings offer a path to greater balance, harmony, and well-being. Their ability to harmonize energies and support spiritual growth makes them an essential component of any holistic healing practice.

The exploration of Tensor Rings and their healing potential is an ongoing journey. As we learn about their effects, we gain new insights into how they influence our lives. From ancient times to today, Tensor

Rings continue to offer hope and healing in a world that is always changing. Their enduring relevance and adaptability highlight the timeless nature of energy healing principles.

Whether used on their own or alongside other healing methods, Tensor Rings have the potential to bring transformation and renewal to those who seek it. By embracing their subtle yet powerful energies, we connect more deeply with the universal forces that shape our existence, guiding us on a journey of healing, growth, and spiritual awakening. Tensor Rings not only enhance our current healing practices but also inspire us to explore new dimensions of energy work, paving the way for a more balanced and harmonious life.

CHAPTER 32:
ORGONE ENERGY

In the world of energy healing, Orgone Energy stands out as a powerful force that helps to create balance, energy, and well-being. When Orgone Energy is present in the Frequency Chamber, it boosts the healing potential of the space, creating a peaceful and supportive environment for transformation and renewal. This enhancement is pivotal in facilitating a deeper and more comprehensive healing experience for all who enter.

So, what exactly is Orgone Energy, and why is it so effective for healing and spiritual growth? To understand Orgone Energy, we need to look at its origins and how it works. Orgone Energy was discovered by Wilhelm Reich, a pioneering psychologist, in the late 1930s. Reich was deeply fascinated by Sigmund Freud's ideas about mental health and sought to explore the basic forces that affect our well-being. Through his extensive research and experiments, Reich identified Orgone Energy as a fundamental life force that is essential for maintaining physical, emotional, and spiritual balance. He termed it "primordial energy," emphasizing its status as a basic and vital force present throughout the universe, permeating all living and non-living matter.

Orgone Energy can be captured and utilized in various ways, such as with devices called orgone accumulators and orgone pyramids. These devices are meticulously crafted from materials like epoxy resin, quartz crystals, and metal shavings, chosen for their specific energetic properties. They work by gathering and directing Orgone Energy to help counteract negative influences and balance out disruptive electromagnetic fields. This process creates an energetically harmonious environment, promoting overall health and well-being.

One of the main benefits of Orgone Energy is its ability to reduce the harmful effects of electromagnetic field (EMF) radiation. This type of radiation emanates from sources like satellites, electrical grids, and everyday electronic devices. Orgone Energy acts as a shield, mitigating these negative effects and creating a protective barrier around individuals. This shielding can lead to improved health, increased energy levels, and enhanced focus, making it an invaluable tool in our increasingly technology-driven world.

People also find that Orgone Energy has a profound positive impact on their mood and emotional well-being. Many individuals report feeling happier, more optimistic, and emotionally balanced after using orgone devices. This uplifted mood can extend to relationships with others, fostering more harmonious and effective interactions with family members, friends, and coworkers. The emotional clarity and stability provided by Orgone Energy contribute significantly to a person's overall sense of happiness and fulfillment.

In the Frequency Chamber, Orgone Energy adds an extra layer to the healing experience. As people relax in the chamber, surrounded by soothing light and calming sound frequencies, the subtle but powerful energy of Orgone Energy fills the space. This infusion creates a balanced and supportive environment for healing and personal growth, allowing individuals to fully immerse themselves in the therapeutic process. The harmonious blend of light, sound, and Orgone Energy works synergistically to enhance the overall effectiveness of the healing modalities used within the chamber.

Orgone Energy also offers practical benefits beyond personal healing. For instance, it has been found to help preserve food. When food is placed on an orgone charging plate, it is believed to stay fresh and retain its nutrients for a longer period. This application contributes to a healthier lifestyle and overall well-being by ensuring that the food we consume remains nutritious and free from spoilage, promoting better health outcomes.

Overall, Orgone Energy is a significant tool for healing and spiritual development. It offers a comprehensive approach to well-being by addressing physical, emotional, and spiritual needs simultaneously. In the Frequency Chamber, Orgone Energy enhances the healing process, promoting deep changes in consciousness and creating a balanced, harmonious environment. This integration of Orgone Energy with other healing modalities underscores its versatility and profound impact on holistic health practices.

The journey of understanding Orgone Energy continues to reveal its many benefits and applications. By exploring and embracing this powerful force, we open ourselves to greater health, vitality, and spiritual growth. Orgone Energy helps us connect more deeply with the universal forces that shape our lives, guiding us toward a more balanced and fulfilling existence. As our knowledge and experience with Orgone Energy expand, so too does our ability to harness its potential, making it an indispensable component of modern energy healing practices.

CHAPTER 33:
SPIRITUAL ALLIES

In the special space of the Frequency Chamber, where soothing sounds mix and healing vibrations fill the air, we connect with realms beyond our usual understanding. This space is more than just a room; it's a sacred sanctuary where we meet spiritual allies—loving beings from different parts of the universe who come to help us heal and grow. This profound connection elevates the healing experience, creating a harmonious blend of energies that facilitate deep transformation.

As the person leading these healing sessions, I see myself as a bridge for these energies. I don't call on these spiritual allies myself; they are naturally drawn to the chamber by the strong presence of light and love that permeates the space. This light and love act like a beacon, guiding them to reach us and offer their unwavering support. The intentional creation of a loving and radiant environment is crucial, as it invites these benevolent beings to participate in our healing journey.

These spiritual allies come from many different backgrounds and have unique roles in our healing journey. They are beings who are dedicated to helping us find balance and transformation. They come with pure intentions, focused on our highest good and our journey toward wholeness. Their diverse origins and specialties enrich the healing process, providing multifaceted support tailored to each individual's needs.

Among the spiritual allies that visit the Frequency Chamber, we often meet Lemurians. These ancient beings are renowned for their deep wisdom and boundless compassion. Their presence helps us feel a strong connection to the earth and its sacred energies. They provide gentle support and nurturing, assisting those who seek healing and spiritual growth by grounding us in the Earth's natural rhythms and fostering a sense of stability and peace.

We also work with Angels, celestial beings made of pure light and love. They fill the chamber with their divine energy, creating a space that feels safe, comforting, and infinitely loving. Their guidance and protection help us stay grounded and calm as we work on our personal healing and growth. Angels offer profound insights and encouragement, uplifting our spirits and reinforcing our sense of purpose and direction.

Another revered group that joins us in the chamber is our Ancestors. These wise guardians connect us to our family's history and heritage, bringing ancestral wisdom and healing. They remind us of our roots and the strength we carry from generations past, providing a sense of continuity and resilience. Their presence honors our lineage and empowers us to draw strength from our heritage as we navigate our healing paths.

There are also Reptilians, beings with a reptilian lineage who come to offer their unique healing gifts. Although they may have a misunderstood reputation, these beings are deeply compassionate and help us understand ourselves better. They guide us in our journey to see our place in the universe more clearly, fostering self-awareness and spiritual insight. Their teachings encourage us to embrace our true nature and align with our higher selves.

As a healer, I feel deeply honored to work with these diverse spiritual allies. Their combined wisdom and support have elevated the healing work in the Frequency Chamber to unprecedented levels. Together, we explore new ways to heal, uncover hidden truths, and support each other in personal growth and transformation. The collaborative energy shared with these allies enhances the effectiveness of our healing sessions, ensuring that each individual receives comprehensive and profound healing.

With the help of these spiritual allies, the Frequency Chamber becomes more than just a physical space. It transforms into a gateway to limitless possibilities and potential. Their presence serves as a constant reminder of the incredible power of love and the universal forces that guide us on our path. This divine partnership fosters a deeper sense of connection and purpose, allowing us to tap into higher states of consciousness and embrace our fullest potential.

As we continue on our journey of healing and personal evolution, let's stay open to the wisdom and guidance of these spiritual allies. Their presence lights our way and fills our hearts with hope and gratitude. Through their love and support, we can discover our true selves and unlock the endless possibilities that lie within us. Embracing these spiritual connections empowers us to navigate life's challenges with grace and resilience, fostering a harmonious and enlightened existence.

By nurturing these relationships with our spiritual allies, we enhance our ability to heal, grow, and transform. The Frequency Chamber stands as a testament to the power of these divine connections, offering a sacred space where love, light, and healing energies converge. Together with our spiritual allies, we embark on a journey of profound healing and spiritual awakening, creating a life of balance, harmony, and infinite potential.

Thomas A. Lewan

Chapter 34:
A Peek into My Healing Session

When you come to a healing session with me, you're about to embark on a journey into the realms of energy, spirit, and deep transformation. I'd like to give you a clear idea of what happens during one of these sessions, how I work, and what incredible experiences might unfold as we spend time together.

When we first sit down, I make sure you understand how the session will go. I want you to know what to expect, fostering a sense of comfort and trust from the very beginning. I explain that I receive information through visions and sometimes through sounds I hear. Sometimes, I might not look directly at you because I'm receiving insights or messages from the spiritual realm. It's like having an ongoing conversation with another world, guiding me as we go. This openness helps create a safe space where you feel supported and understood.

I also prepare you for any physical sensations you

171

might feel during the session. You might experience vibrations, tingling, or even emotional releases like laughter or tears. These are completely natural and part of the healing process. It's a sign that something deep within you is shifting and changing, allowing you to release old energies and embrace new ones. Understanding these sensations helps you stay present and engaged in your healing journey.

As we talk about your experiences, I start to sense what's happening inside your body. It's like my senses become tuned in to your energy, picking up subtle cues that reveal more about your state of being. I might see details like your bone structure, scars from past relationships or losses, or even signs of old injuries. Sometimes, I get insights into the state of your blood, giving me a deeper understanding of your physical and energetic health. These observations are not just visual; they are accompanied by a deep intuitive knowing that guides the session towards areas needing attention.

We often dive into these observations, discussing what I perceive and how it relates to your overall well-being. I believe in blending spiritual insights with scientific understanding to help empower you on your healing journey. This approach bridges the gap between the mystical and the practical, making the process more relatable and meaningful. By integrating these perspectives, we can address both the tangible and intangible aspects of your health, ensuring a comprehensive healing experience.

When you lie down for the session, I place my hands

on your feet. In this position, your entire body seems to light up for me. It's as if your energy field becomes a canvas, ready to be filled with healing and guidance. This is when spiritual guides and masters often make their presence known, drawn to the shifts in your energy. Their presence adds a layer of divine support, enhancing the healing vibrations that flow through me.

Sometimes, you might feel spiritual presences around you, but you might not receive clear messages. In these cases, I help invite only the most relevant guides and masters. We focus on quality over quantity, ensuring that the guidance you receive is meaningful and useful for your healing journey. This selective invitation process maintains the purity and intention of the healing environment, allowing for a more focused and effective session.

Throughout the session, we work on changing the energy in the room, raising its vibration, and clearing away any negative or stagnant energies. This allows the healing energy to flow freely without being blocked by energetic debris. You might notice a distinct shift in the energy of the space during this phase, feeling lighter and more at peace as the environment becomes more conducive to healing.

Occasionally, departed loved ones may come through during the session. This can be comforting, showing that they are still present and watching over you. I describe their energy as best I can, focusing on details like the feel of their presence or their unique energy signature. However, I don't present myself as a psychic medium to avoid putting pressure on you to make specific connections with the departed. The main goal is to facilitate healing and transformation, not to provide specific messages from loved ones.

While I do work on your chakras, I don't always see them in color during the session. Instead, I rely on physical sensations and intuitive feelings to understand each chakra's state. I only see their colors toward the end of the session when I take a moment to assess their vibrational levels. This subtle awareness allows me to address imbalances effectively, ensuring that each energy center is aligned and functioning optimally.

One thing I emphasize is that the visions you might experience during the session aren't always meant to be taken literally. They're more like messages in the form of images that carry healing frequencies. It's important not to overanalyze these visions or fixate on what you see. They serve as tools for transformation and healing, not as literal answers. Embracing this perspective helps you stay open to the healing process without becoming attached to specific outcomes.

As we wrap up the session, I make sure you leave with a strong sense of connection, healing, and empowerment. I remind you that healing is a continuous process, and I'm here to support you as you continue your journey toward better well-being. This closing phase often includes grounding exercises and affirmations to help you integrate the healing energy into your daily life, ensuring that the benefits of the session extend beyond our time together.

These sessions are more than just a way to heal; they're about reconnecting with your true self, understanding how all aspects of your life are connected, and embracing the profound changes that come from opening yourself to the wisdom and guidance of the spiritual realm. Each session is a step toward greater self-awareness and holistic well-being, empowering you to live a more balanced and fulfilling life.

By sharing this glimpse into my healing sessions, I hope you feel more prepared and inspired to embark on your own healing journey. Trust in the process, embrace the experiences, and allow the transformative power of energy and spirit to guide you toward profound healing and personal growth.

Through the Eyes of an Energy Healer

CHAPTER 35:
HOW I SEE ENERGY

Understanding energy is like looking into a hidden world that lies beneath our everyday lives. This world is full of vibrations, frequencies, and patterns that shape how we experience things, think, and feel. When I look at someone's energy field, it's not just a vague concept but a real phenomenon made up of these complex energy frequencies. This intricate tapestry of energy provides a deeper insight into a person's overall well-being and state of balance.

For me, seeing energy isn't quite like the usual pictures of auras and chakras with bright, colorful lights. Instead, I perceive energy in shades of white and gray. Overlaid on this, I notice what I can only describe as small orange numbers. These numbers represent different frequencies, and they pulse and shift around in a person's energy field. Each frequency carries its own special information, and I often ask Spirit for more details about what these frequencies signify. This numerical aspect adds a unique layer to my understanding, allowing me to decode the subtle messages embedded within the energy.

When I talk to someone, their energy field changes right in front of me. It's like the little orange numbers start to arrange themselves into sentences and paragraphs of information. This transformation indicates that deeper spiritual insights or guidance are being shared. It's a powerful moment when the energy around a person becomes a conduit for understanding more profoundly. These dynamic shifts provide real-time feedback on the person's emotional and spiritual state, enhancing the healing process.

Inside a person's energy field, I see many layers, each with its own frequency. Sometimes these layers resemble translucent veils that move like smoke. Each layer has its own energy, swirling in different directions and sometimes changing colors. My job is to help these layers work together in harmony, almost like conducting an orchestra where each part comes together to create a beautiful symphony. This orchestration ensures that the energy flows smoothly, promoting balance and preventing stagnation.

These frequencies and layers of energy hold everything about a person's life. Every thought, idea, and interaction leaves a mark in the energy field, creating a living record of their experiences. When we interact with others, whether through talking or just being in the same space, our energies mix and affect each other. It's a constant exchange of information happening on many levels, influencing our moods, behaviors, and overall health.

When I connect with Spirit, it's like tuning a radio to a higher frequency. To reach this spiritual level, I need to raise my own vibration, which helps me access deeper insights and knowledge. As I adjust to this higher frequency, I notice that the frequencies in a person's energy field become more vivid and lively, as if they are reacting to the presence of Spirit. This elevated state enhances the clarity and depth of the healing session, making the insights more profound and impactful.

During a session, my goal is to create a strong connection between the client and the spiritual realm. This connection often leads to changes in the energy frequencies in their auric field. It's like seeing a symphony of energies coming into balance, with each part playing a role in the overall pattern of the person's life. This harmonious balance facilitates healing, allowing for the release of negative energies and the infusion of positive, revitalizing vibrations.

Even though I can see these frequencies and energy layers, I often choose not to make direct eye contact during a session. Instead, I concentrate on the information and insights that Spirit is sharing with me. I've learned to trust this method and let Spirit guide my work. I don't need to focus on the physical details of the person because I'm tuned into their energetic essence. This focused attention on the spiritual and energetic aspects ensures that the healing process is intuitive and deeply aligned with the client's needs.

As I work with clients, my main aim is to empower

them and provide clarity and healing. I encourage them to set aside their expectations and let Spirit lead the session. By going with the spiritual flow, the most profound changes and healing can happen. This approach fosters a sense of trust and openness, allowing clients to fully embrace the healing journey and experience meaningful transformation.

In a world where energy is usually invisible, I've been given a special way of seeing things. I perceive the dance of frequencies, the harmony of energies, and the deep potential for healing and transformation that exists within each person. This ability is both a gift and a privilege, and I use it to help others on their journeys of self-discovery and healing. By understanding and interpreting these subtle energy patterns, I guide my clients toward greater harmony, balance, and well-being, fostering a deeper connection with their true selves and the universal energies that sustain us all.

CHAPTER 36:
EMBRACING GROWTH AND
EVOLUTION IN HEALING

In the grand story of life, growth is not just a choice but a natural part of our journey. It's woven into every moment of our existence, shaping who we are and who we become. My own path in healing is a perfect example of this. It's been a journey filled with deep changes, growth, and new discoveries, each step building upon the last to create a tapestry of personal and spiritual evolution.

Thinking back to the start of my journey, I remember how simple things used to be. I recall how even a small moment, like noticing the Geico lizard, felt significant. In those early days, every experience, no matter how ordinary it seemed, had the potential to bring new insights and awakenings. These seemingly mundane moments were actually seeds of profound transformation, planting the groundwork for my future growth.

As I moved forward in my healing practice, I embraced each chance for growth with an open heart and a readiness to learn. Each day, I explored the mysteries of the spiritual world more deeply, refining my intuitive skills and broadening my understanding of energy healing. This continuous learning process not only enhanced my abilities but also deepened my connection to the universal energies that guide us all.

As time went on, I realized that I wasn't alone in my healing work. I started to feel the presence of multiple spirit guides joining me in my sessions. Their presence brought wisdom, guidance, and healing energy that went beyond what I could offer on my own. With their help, I witnessed amazing changes and miracles that seemed to go beyond the physical world's limitations. These spirit guides became invaluable companions on my journey, offering support and insights that accelerated my growth and healing capabilities.

One of the most important moments in my journey came when I was given the guidance to create something as intricate and powerful as the Frequency Chamber. This special place, inspired by divine wisdom and guided by spirit, symbolizes the incredible potential within all of us to create and bring our deepest visions to life. The Frequency Chamber stands as a testament to the synergy between human intention and spiritual guidance, embodying the essence of holistic healing.

As I continued to grow, I felt a strong pull to expand my healing practice. I envisioned a place called Rare Earth Rock Shop and Holistic Wellness Center. This would be a special space where healing, spirituality, and holistic wellness could come together harmoniously. With determination and the support of spirit, I began working to make this vision a reality. The creation of Rare Earth Rock Shop and Holistic Wellness Center was a significant milestone, representing the culmination of years of dedication and spiritual alignment.

Today, Rare Earth Rock Shop and Holistic Wellness Center is a beacon of healing and transformation in Dickinson, ND. It stands as proof of what can be achieved with clear intentions, hard work, and trust in the divine flow of life. Within its walls, people from all walks of life find comfort, healing, and guidance on their paths of self-discovery and spiritual awakening. This space not only serves as a center for healing but also as a community hub where individuals can connect, share, and grow together.

Through everything, one truth has always been clear: growth is a fundamental part of life. Just like a seed grows into a plant in fertile soil, we all have the natural ability to grow and flourish according to our deepest desires and intentions. As I continue my healing journey, I am reminded each day of the wisdom that comes from letting life flow and allowing spirit to guide me. Embracing this natural progression fosters resilience, adaptability, and a deeper sense of purpose.

Every morning, as I wake up to a new day, I offer a prayer of thanks for the journey that has led me here. With an open heart and a readiness to embrace the unknown, I ask Spirit what wonders the day might bring.

In that simple act of surrender, I find myself wrapped in the ongoing mystery of life, ready to welcome whatever blessings and challenges come my way as I continue to grow and evolve in my healing journey. This daily practice of gratitude and openness reinforces my commitment to continual growth, ensuring that I remain aligned with my highest self and the universal energies that support my evolution.

By embracing growth and evolution, I honor the dynamic nature of life and the endless possibilities that lie ahead. This commitment to personal and spiritual development not only enhances my own healing journey but also empowers those I work with to embark on their own paths of transformation and self-discovery.

CHAPTER 37:
THE BOTTOM LINE

At the core of everything in life is energy. It's a fundamental truth that often goes unnoticed. Everything around us, from the chair we sit on to the thoughts we think, is a form of energy. Understanding this concept is crucial because it unlocks our potential for transformation and healing, allowing us to harness the power within ourselves to create positive changes in our lives.

Our thoughts are a powerful form of energy. They can impact our mental and emotional states, and even our physical health. This idea is connected to something called the placebo effect. When people take a pill with no active ingredients but believe it will work, they often experience real improvements in their condition. This shows how our beliefs and expectations can affect our health, even when there's no real medicine involved. The mind's ability to influence the body highlights the profound connection between our mental states and physical well-being.

Imagine a doctor telling a patient they have a terminal illness and only six months to live. If the patient believes this diagnosis, their body might start to respond as if the prediction is true. This demonstrates how strong our thoughts and beliefs can be—they can become self-fulfilling prophecies, shaping our reality in ways we might not fully comprehend.

In clinical studies, people who were given placebos instead of real medication sometimes experienced side effects just like those listed for the actual medication. Some lost their hair, others lost weight, and some even had skin issues—all because they believed they might experience these effects. This illustrates how our thoughts can influence our physical bodies, creating real physiological responses based purely on belief. The power of the mind is evident in how it can manifest changes in the body, underscoring the importance of maintaining a positive and focused mindset.

The connection between mind and body is profound. It's not just a phrase; it's a real and powerful aspect of human existence. Our thoughts can shape our experiences, both positively and negatively. Many people don't fully appreciate how they can use their thoughts for healing and personal growth, often overlooking the immense potential they hold to influence their own lives.

One effective practice is visualization. When we visualize something with detail and intention, we tap into our mind's creative power. It's not just about imagining a picture; it's about feeling the experience as if it's happening. For example, if you want to visit Hawaii, don't just put a picture of it on your vision board. Instead, imagine the details: the travel agency you'll visit, the name of the travel agent, the airline you'll choose, your seat on the plane, the meal you'll enjoy, and the view from your hotel room. Creating a vivid mental image sends a strong message to the universe about your desires, making your intentions clearer and more compelling.

Visualization is more than just daydreaming; it's about aligning your thoughts, emotions, and energy with what you want. When you do this with clarity and enthusiasm, you signal to the universe that you're ready to receive your desires. The more you feel like your vision is real, the closer it gets to becoming a reality. This practice reinforces the power of positive thinking and intentional creation, enabling you to manifest your goals and dreams effectively.

Here's a simple truth: if you wait until you achieve your goals to feel successful, you might always be chasing them. But if you embrace the feeling of success now, you'll notice a shift in your energy. This shift can attract more abundance and fulfillment into your life. By embodying the emotions associated with your desired outcomes, you create a magnetic energy that draws those outcomes into your reality, fostering a proactive and empowered approach to achieving your goals.

The mind's influence on the body goes beyond positive thinking. During World War II, when morphine was unavailable, soldiers were given saline solution but were told it was morphine. Surprisingly, they felt pain relief similar to what real morphine would provide. This shows the incredible power of belief, as the mind can trigger physiological responses that mimic actual medical treatments. The placebo effect remains a testament to the mind's capacity to influence the body's healing processes, highlighting the need to cultivate strong, positive beliefs for optimal health.

In another study, participants were divided into two groups. One group did physical exercises, while the other group only visualized doing the exercises. Remarkably, the group that only imagined the exercises saw a 7.83% increase in muscle mass, even without physically working out. This demonstrates that the body responds to the mind's intentions, whether they are acted out or simply visualized. Such findings emphasize the profound connection between mental focus and physical development, showcasing the potential for mental practices to induce tangible physical changes.

Understanding that our thoughts shape our reality is essential. Negative thoughts, such as self-doubt or criticism, can release stress hormones that interfere with the body's healing processes. On the other hand, positive thoughts and beliefs can trigger healing chemicals that support overall well-being. This duality underscores the importance of cultivating a positive mental environment to foster health and resilience, enabling us to navigate life's challenges with greater ease and confidence.

So, the bottom line is this: our thoughts are powerful creators of our reality. They can uplift us or bring us down. They influence our health and determine our success. It's up to us to harness this incredible power, recognize the potential for transformation and healing in our thoughts, and use this knowledge to create the lives we truly want. The mind is a powerful force, and it's time we learn to use it consciously and positively as we navigate through life. By understanding and applying the principles of energy and thought, we can unlock our full potential and lead more fulfilling, balanced lives.

Discover deeper insights and personal reflections straight from the author! Scan the QR code to explore the wisdom behind the words.

.